SUPERIOR COURT OF LAW AND EQUITY
MERO DISTRICT OF TENNESSEE
1810-1813

(MIDDLE TENNESSEE)

Abstracted by Mary Sue Smith

HERITAGE BOOKS
2006

HERITAGE BOOKS
AN IMPRINT OF HERITAGE BOOKS, INC.

Books, CDs, and more—Worldwide

For our listing of thousands of titles see our website
at
www.HeritageBooks.com

Published 2006 by
HERITAGE BOOKS, INC.
Publishing Division
65 East Main Street
Westminster, Maryland 21157-5026

Copyright © 2006 Mary Sue Smith

All rights reserved. No part of this book may be reproduced or transmitted in any form or by any means, electronic or mechanical, including photocopying, recording or by any information storage and retrieval system without written permission from the author, except for the inclusion of brief quotations in a review.

International Standard Book Number: 978 -0-7884-4090-X

MERO DISTRICT SUPERIOR COURT
1810 – 1813

This book is the third in a series of surviving docket books for the Mero District Superior Court beginning with the March Term 1810. This docket book is at the Metro/Davidson County Archives.

The importance of this information is that the people named cover all the area of what is now known as Middle Tennessee.[1] Many of the people named may not be found in other documents.

The Superior Courts of Law and Equity had sole jurisdiction over cases punishable by loss of life or limb and cases of greater dollar value as well as appeals for those dissatisfied with a Court of Pleas decision. The County Court of Common Pleas and Quarter Sessions handled cases involving less than fifty dollars in property or fines. In this period the three traveling Superior Court judges heard cases in Jonesboro (Washington District), Knoxville (Hamilton District), Carthage (Winchester District), Clarksville (Robertson District) and Nashville (Mero District).[2]

In 1809 the legislature formed a Circuit Court, to be held in each county. The Superior Court was renamed the Supreme Court of Errors and Appeals. In this book you will find cases assigned to the various County Circuit Courts or to a different Superior Court District, so if this is the person you are researching you can now search for the appropriate County Circuit Court Minute Book to find further information.

The surviving loose papers for the Superior Court were transferred to the new Supreme Court and may be found at the Tennessee Library and Archives with the Supreme Court records.

---

[1] *A History of the Courts of Davidson County*, George L. Rooker, Circuit Court Clerk [Handbook for jurors].

[2] *Tennessee Court System Prior to 1870*, Charles A. Sherrill, 1998 (article), TNGenNet.Inc.

MERO DISTRICT SUPERIOR COURT - 1810 - 1813

Page	Case #	Surname	Given name	Title	Action/Pleas	Date	Orders of Court
p1	#1	Herrod	Barned	plaintiff	covenant	March 1810	cont'd
p1	#1	Hays	Robert	defendant		Sept 1810	cont'd
p1						March 1811	cont'd
p1					declaration	Sept 1811	cont'd
p1					demurrer & joinder	March 1812	Dem. sustained
p1							pltf pay cost
p1							
p1	#2	Maxwell	Jesse	plaintiff	covenant declaration	March 1810	cont'd
p1	#2	Molloy	Thomas, executors	defendant	demurrer & joinder	Sept 1810	cont'd
p1						March 1811	cont'd
p1						Sept 1811	cont'd
p1						March 1812	demurrer sustained/judg
p1							pltf pay costs
p1	#3	Sneed	William	plaintiff	petition	March 1810	cont'd
p1	#3	Hooper	Joseph & wife	defendant	answer & replication	Sept 1810	cont'd

MERO DISTRICT SUPERIOR COURT - 1810 - 1813

p1						March 1811	cont'd
p1						Sept 1811	cont'd
p1						March 1812	deft pay petitioner $120.50/ petitioner pay costs for his witnesses/ deft pay rest
p1							
p1							
p1							
p1	#4	Kiefe	Margaret	plaintiff	petition for divorce	March 1810	cont'd
p1	#4	Kiefe	Thomas	defendant		Sept 1810	cont'd
p1						March 1811	jury/ deft guilty in 1st issue/cont'd
p1						March 1812	cont'd
p1						Sept 1812	decree //be divorced//Thomas pay costs
p2	#5	Clark	David	plaintiff	case/set off & issue	March 1810	cont'd
p2	#5	Hamilton	James	defendant		Sept 1810	cont'd
p2						March 1811	Nonsuit/judg for costs
p2	#6	Copeland	Samuel	plaintiff	certiorari	March 1810	cont'd
p2	#6	Scott	William, Senr	defendant		Sept 1810	cont'd

MERO DISTRICT SUPERIOR COURT - 1810 - 1813

p2						March 1812	cont'd
p2						Sept 1812	motion to dismiss overruled
p2						Dec 1812	jury/find for defendant/judg for costs
p2							
p2	#7	Oren	James	plaintiff	Scifa surrender to sheriff	March 1810	cont'd
p2	#7	Maclin	John	deft bail		Sept 1810	jury/juror withdrawn/cont'd
p2	#7	Bean	Stephen	defendant		March 1811	cont'd
p2						Sept 1811	jury/mistrial/cont'd
p2						March 1812	jury/say did not surrender Bean to shff
p2						Sept 1812	judgt for pltf for $194.40 & interest since 10 May 1806 + costs
p2							
p2							
p2	#8	Kincaid	John	plaintiff	debt appeal	March 1810	cont'd
p2	#8	Francis	Thomas W.	deft/admr		Sept 1810	by consent adjourned to the next court of errors & appeals of the 4th circuit
p2	#8	Thomas	Robert	deceased			
p3	#9	Maclin	John	plaintiff	in error	March 1810	cont'd
p3	#9	Ferguson	Thomas S.	defendant		Sept 1810	judg of the county court affirmed

MERO DISTRICT SUPERIOR COURT   -   1810 - 1813

p3							with ... interest & costs
p3							
p3	#10	Demumbrune	Timothy	plaintiff	case appeal	March 1810	cont'd
p3	#10	Betts	William	defendant		Sept 1810	cont'd / deposition
p3	#10	Stothart	R.	witness	deposition/Nashville	March 1811	jury/mistrial/cont'd
p3					5 days notice	Sept 1811	jury/find for pltf/rule by deft for new trial
p3							deft filed bill of exceptions//to the next
p3							court of errors & appeals for 4th circuit
p3							
p3	#11	Brooks	William	plaintiff	debt	March 1810	cont'd
p3	#11	McKean	Joseph	defendant		Sept 1810	cont'd
p3						March 1811	cont'd on afft of pet.
p3						Sept 1811	jury/finds in favor of defendant/
p3							defendant may recover his costs
p3							pltf files writ of exception/writ of error to
p3							next Supreme Ct of Writs & Appeals to
p3							the Circuit Ct of the 4th Circuit
p3						Sept 1812	suit remands to Circuit Ct/new trial
p3						Dec 1812	nonsuit/judgment for costs
p3							

MERO DISTRICT SUPERIOR COURT - 1810 - 1813

p3	#12	Irwin	John	plaintiff	debt appeal	March 1810	cont'd
p3	#12	Hickman	Thomas	defendant	covenants performed	Sept 1810	cont'd
p3						March 1811	cont'd
p3						Sept 1811	cont'd
p3						March 1812	cont'd
p3						Sept 1812	deft dem. to pltf overruled/new trial
p3						May 1813	jury finds for deft/judgment & costs
p4	#13	Foster	Anthony	plaintiff	in error	March 1810	cont'd
p4	#13	Francis	Charles	defendant	errors assigned	Sept 1810	judg. of the Co.Ct reviewed/new trial ordered
p4							in the County Court/Anthony recover his costs
p4							
p4	#14	Jackson	Samuel	plaintiff	in error	March 1810	cont'd
p4	#14	Jackson	Andrew	defendant	errors assigned	Sept 1810	Dem. sustained//judgment of the County
p4	#14	Hutchings	John	defendant	Dem./assign. of errors		Court affirmed
p4							
p4	#15	Hunt	William	plaintiff	case appeal	March 1810	cont'd

MERO DISTRICT SUPERIOR COURT - 1810 - 1813

p4	#15	Bell	Montgomery	defendant	non asst & issue	Sept 1810	cont'd
p4	#15	Searcy	Robert	pltfs agent		March 1811	cont'd on afft of agent for pltf
p4						Sept 1811	cont'd
p4						March 1812	cont'd
p4						Dec 1812	cont'd
p4						May 1813	jury/ find for deft/ judg for costs
p4							
p4	#16	Stump	Christopher	plaintiff	case appeal	March 1810	cont'd
p4	#16	Skinner	Nathan	defendant		Sept 1810	cont'd
p4	#16	Stump	John	pltfs agent		March 1811	cont'd on afft of agent for pltf
p4						Sept 1811	cont'd
p4						March 1812	jury//find for defendant/judg for costs
p5	#17	Thompson	Neil	plaintiff	debt appeal	March 1810	cont'd
p5	#17	Hinton	Jeremiah	defendant	payment set off	Sept 1810	cont'd on afft of deft
p5					issues	March 1811	jury/sat deft has paid $231.31 part of the debt
p5							... assess pltfs damages to $39.77 besides

MERO DISTRICT SUPERIOR COURT - 1810 - 1813

p5							his costs//judgment of Co.Ct confirmed
p5							
p5	#18	Sheppard	Jacob	plaintiff	case appeal	March 1810	cont'd
p5	#18	Stump	Christopher	defendant	not guilty & issue	Sept 1810	cont'd
p5						March 1811	cont on afft of agent for deft
p5						Sept 1811	cont'd
p5						March 1812	jury/ find for pltf & assess his damage to $400
p5							judg for the same & costs//deft files bills of
p5							exception which are allowed
p5						Sept 1812	suit remanded to circuit court & new trial
p5						Dec 1812	cont'd by consent
p5						May 1813	cause removed
p5							
p5	#19	Napier	Richard	plaintiff	covenant	March 1810	cont'd
p5	#19	Wills	Benjamin D.	deft/exor	non est factum & issue	Sept 1810	cont'd
p5	#19	Wills	Elias	deceased	fully administered	March 1811	by consent cont to next term..pltf pay costs
					rept & issue	Sept 1811	deft comes into court & confesses judgment
p5							for $1,000 & costs ...
p5							

MERO DISTRICT SUPERIOR COURT   -   1810 - 1813

p5							
p5	#20	Marr	George W. L.	plaintiff	case certiorari	March 1810	cont'd
p5	#20	Renfro	Robert	defendant	non assumset & set off	Sept 1810	order of reference set aside & cont'd
p5	#20	Thomas	Robert	witness		March 1811	jury//find for deft//deft to pay allowance for
p5	#20	Wharton	Jesse	witness			witnesses
p5	#20	Dickinson	Jno	witness			
p6	#21	Overton	Thomas J.	plaintiff	certiorari	March 1810	cont'd
p6	#21	Trimble	David	constable		Sept 1810	cont'd
p6	#21	Trimble	John	security		March 1811	cont'd
p6	#21	Brown	Joseph	security		Sept 1811	ordered suit be dismissed unless pltf give
p6							security before next court//cont'd
p6						March 1812	pltf has not given security//suit dismissed
p6							ordered pltf pay the costs
p6							
p6	#22	Witherspoon	John	case	case	March 1810	cont'd
p6	#22	Shute	John		non asst & issue	Sept 1810	cont'd//deft to take deposition
p6	#22	Shute	Isaac	witness	deposition - 10 days	March 1811	cont'd by consent

MERO DISTRICT SUPERIOR COURT   -   1810 - 1813

p6	#22	Childress	Henry	witness	deposition	Sept 1811	cont'd//deft to take deposition
p6						March 1812	jury//find for pltf & assess damages $430.68
p6							rule by deft to have new trial // cont'd
p6						Sept 1812	new trial granted//deft to pay costs last term
p6						Dec 1812	cont'd on afft of the plaintiff
p6						May 1813	jury//find for pltf//$648.10 & costs
p6							writ of error granted & security
p6							
p6	#23	Den	John	pltf/lessee	ejectment	March 1810	cont'd
p6	#23	Alexander	Parker & als	owner	not guilty & issue	Sept 1810	cont'd
p6	#23	Bland	Arthur	defendant		March 1811	cont'd on afft of agent for defendant
p6						Sept 1811	cont'd
p6						March 1812	jury//deft is not guilty//judg for deft
p6							pltf files bill of exceptions & obtains a writ of
p6							error to the next Supreme Ct of Errors &
p6							Appeals for the 4th Circuit
p6							
p6	#24	Campbell	John	plaintiff	covenant appeal	March 1810	cont'd

MERO DISTRICT SUPERIOR COURT - 1810 - 1813

p6	#24	Jackson	Andrew	deft/exor	fully admd & repn, issue	Sept 1810	cont'd
p6	#24	Hutchings	John	deft/exor	non .. & issue	March 1811	cont'd
p6	#24	Hutchings	Thos.	deceased	cov't perf'd & issue	Sept 1811	cont'd
p6					special plea, Demurrer	March 1812	cont'd
p6					& joinder	Sept 1812	cont'd
p6						Dec 1812	cont'd
						March 1813	Nonsuit//judgt for costs
p7	#25	Marr	George W. L.	plaintiff	debt appeal	March 1810	cont'd
p7	#25	Gordon	John	defendant	payment repn & issue	Sept 1810	jury//find for pltf $438.90 // judg for the
p7							county confirmed
p7							
p7	#26	Bedford	John R.	plaintiff	in error/errors assigned	March 1810	cont'd
p7	#26	Perkins	Thomas H.	defendant		Sept 1810	cert awarded deft for a more complete copy of
p7							the judg of the county court//judgment of the
p7							county court affirmed with 6% interest
p7							

10

MERO DISTRICT SUPERIOR COURT - 1810 - 1813

p7	#27	Stump	John	plaintiff	in error/errors assigned	March 1810	cont'd
p7	#27	Smith	John H. & Co.	defendant		Sept 1810	judgment of the county court affirmed with
p7							12% interest & costs
p7	#28	Beck	John	plaintiff	in error/errors assigned	March 1810	cont'd
p7	#28	King, Carson & King		defendant		Sept 1810	death of Wm & James King suggested
p7	#28	King	Wm	deceased			judg of the county court affirmed with 6% int.
p7	#28	King	James	deceased			
p8	#29	Reed	Moses	plaintiff	debt appl	March 1810	cont'd
p8	#29	Tyrrell	James	deft/admr	payment & issue	Sept 1810	cont'd by consent/adm to plead at next court
p8	#29	Kerr	Sam'l	deceased		March 1811	right to plead waived & deft confessed judg.
p8	#29	Harney	Thomas	deceased			for the amount of the judg in county court with
p8							12% interest from day of county ct judg.
p8							
p8	#30	Reed	Moses	plaintiff	debt appeal	March 1810	cont'd
p8	#30	Tyrrell	James	deft/admr	payment & issue	Sept 1810	cont'd by consent/ admr to plead at next court
p8	#30	Kerr	Sam'l	deceased		March 1811	right to plead waived by consent & deft

MERO DISTRICT SUPERIOR COURT - 1810 - 1813

p8	#30	Harney	Thomas	deceased				confesses judg. for the amount of the judg. in
p8								the co. ct. with 12% interest
p8								
p8	#31	Watkins	Thomas G.	plaintiff	case appeal	March 1810	cont'd	
p8	#31	Catlett	Hanson	defendant	non asst & issue	Sept 1810	cont'd	
p8						March 1811	cont'd	
p8						Sept 1811	cont'd	
p8						March 1812	cont'd by consent	
p8						Sept 1812	cont'd	
p8						Dec 1812	cont'd by consent	
p8						May 1813	jury//find for pltf & ass. dam. to $120 & costs	
p8								
p8	#32	Kavanaugh	Charles	plaintiff	debt appeal	March 1810	cont'd	
p8	#32	McDaniel	Clement	defendant	payment & issue	Sept 1810	jury//find for pltf $127.13 & 12% interest	
p8								
p9	#33	King, Carson & King		plaintiff	debt appeal	March 1810	cont'd	

MERO DISTRICT SUPERIOR COURT - 1810 - 1813

p9	#33	Shute	Thomas	defendant	payment & issue	Sept 1810	the death of Wm & James King suggested
p9	#33	King	Wm	deceased			jury//find for pltf $222.71/12% interest
p9	#33	King	James	deceased			
p9							
p9	#34	Edmondson	William	plaintiff	in error	March 1810	cont'd
p9	#34	Stephens	Lewis	defendant	errors assigned	Sept 1810	jury//find the issue for deft in error
p9							judgt of the county court affirmed
p9							
p9	#35	Cockrill	John, Junr	plaintiff	covenant appeal	March 1810	cont'd
p9	#35	Reaves	Robert	defendant	declaration dem & joinder	Sept 1810	cont'd
p9					writ of enquiry	March 1811	cont'd
p9						Sept 1811	Demurrer overruled/writ of enq. awarded/cont'd
p9						March 1812	jury//find the damage sustained to $365.84
p9							
p9	#36	Burnett	George	plaintiff	case appeal	March 1810	cont'd
p9	#36	Raymond	Nicholas	plaintiff	non asst & issue	Sept 1810	cont'd
p9	#36	Stothart	Robert	defendant		March 1811	jury//find for pltf //damages to $1355.00 & cost
p9							judgment of the county court affirmed

MERO DISTRICT SUPERIOR COURT - 1810 - 1813

p10	#37	Phillips	Charles S.	plaintiff	case	March 1810	cont'd
p10	#37	Sayers	Sampson	defendant	non assumpset & issue	Sept 1810	cont'd
p10						March 1811	Nonsuit // judgment for costs
p10							
p10	#38	Deaderick & Sommerville		plaintiff	debt cert.	March 1810	cont'd
p10	#38	Anderson	Patton	defendant	payment	Sept 1810	jury//find for pltf//$83.60
p10	#38	Coleman	Joseph	defendant	& issue		judgment of county court affirmed
p10							
p10	#39	Gray	Suckey	pltf/exor	debt	March 1810	cont'd
p10	#39	Gray	Young A.	pltf/exor	special plea	Sept 1810	cont'd
p10	#39	Gray	James	deceased	repn & issue	March 1811	jury//find for pltf//damages $1329.65 & costs
p10	#39	Robertson	James	defendant			judgment for the same & costs
p10							
p10	#40	Wiggins	Joseph & als	plaintiff	ejectment	March 1810	cont'd
p10	#40	Rains	John	defendant		Sept 1810	cont'd by consent/land to be surveyed
p10	#40	Childs	John	defendant		March 1811	cont'd

MERO DISTRICT SUPERIOR COURT - 1810 - 1813

p10	#40	Westley	Sam'l	surveyor		Sept 1811	jury//Nonsuit judgment for costs
p11	#41	Williams	Daniel	plaintiff	debt appeal	March 1810	cont'd
p11	#41	Stump	Christopher	defendant		Sept 1811	cont'd
p11	#41	Williams	O.	pltfs agent		March 1811	jury//Nonsuit //set aside//new trial next ct
p11						Sept 1811	cont'd
p11						March 1812	jury//find for pltf//debt $50.00//cont'd
p11						Sept 1812	new trial granted//deft to pay costs last term
p11						Dec 1812	dismissed by pltfs agent//share costs
p11							
p11	#42	Jackson	Andrew	plaintiff	covn't appeal	March 1810	cont'd
p11	#42	Jackson	Samuel	defendant	cov't perf'd	Sept 1810	jury// find for pltf // damages to $67.90
p11							
p11	#43	Champ	John	pltf/guardian	cov't appeal	March 1810	cont'd
p11	#43	Sanders	Edward	defendant	cov't perf'd	Sept 1810	cont'd
p11					rep'n & issues	March 1811	cont'd

MERO DISTRICT SUPERIOR COURT - 1810 - 1813

p11						Sept 1811	cont'd
p11						March 1812	pltf demurrers to defts plea sustained
p11						Sept 1812	jury//find for pltf//damages to $142
p11							
p11	#44	Johnston	Andrew	plaintiff	case appeal	March 1810	cont'd
p11	#44	Lewis	Joel	plaintiff	dem & joinder	Sept 1810	Demurrer overruled & writ of enquiry awarded
p11	#44	Waggeman	Thomas	defendant	writ of enquiry	March 1811	cont'd
p11	#44	Lytle	William	defendant		Sept 1811	jury//say pltf has sustained damages of
p11							$466.30
p12	#45	Trammell	Garrard	plaintiff	scifa appeal	March 1810	cont'd
p12	#45	Jackson	James	bail	paymt/issue	Sept 1810	cont'd
p12	#45	Cribbins	William	defendant	dem & joinder	March 1811	cont'd
p12						Sept 1811	cont'd by consent
p12						March 1812	jury/find deft has not paid debt in scifa/Dem cont'd
p12						Sept 1812	dem error overruled & judg of CoCt affirmed

MERO DISTRICT SUPERIOR COURT - 1810 - 1813

p12					covenant	March	
p12	#46	Napier	Thomas	plaintiff	appeal	1810	cont'd
p12	#46	Phillips	Benjamin	defendant	cov't performed	Sept 1810	cont'd
p12	#46	Crutcher	Thos	umpire		March 1811	cont'd
p12	#46	Scales	Jos.	umpire		Sept 1811	cont'd by consent
p12						March 1812	cont'd by consent
p12						Sept 1812	cont'd
p12						Dec 1812	referred to umpires/judg of umpires to be judg/t
p12						May 1813	judg/t for pltf on arbitration//$76 & costs
p12							
p12	#47			pltf/lessee	eject. appeal	March 1810	cont'd
p12	#47	Sapping	Roger B.	owner	not guilty/issue	Sept 1810	jury/defts not guilty of trespass & eject
p12	#47	Owen	Edmond	defendant			judgment for costs
p12	#47	Drury	Richard	defendant			
p12							
p12	#48	Wood	Samuel	pltf/adm	case appeal	March 1810	cont'd
p12	#48	Janny	Abel	deceased	dem & joinder	Sept 1810	cont'd

MERO DISTRICT SUPERIOR COURT - 1810 - 1813

p12	#48	Dillon	William	defendant		March 1811	cont'd	
p12	#48	Dillon	Isaac	admr		Sept 1811	cont'd	
p12	#48	Dillon	Nathan	admr		March 1812	deft being dead, ordered scifa be issued to admrs	
p12							Scifa executed July 1st 1812	
p12						Sept 1812	deft being dead & no steps taken for 2 terms of	
p12							court ordered suit be abated	
p13	#49	Wood	Samuel	pltf/adm			duplicate of previous case #48	
p13	#49	Janny	Abel	deceased				
p13	#49	Dillon	William	defendant				
p13								
p13	#50	Nash	William	plaintiff	scifa appeal	March 1810	cont'd	
p13	#50	Nichols	John	defts bail	plea by Nichols	Sept 1810	jury/find deft has not paid the debt/judg for amount	
p13	#50	Germain	William	defts bail	pay't & issue		of judg't in county court with 12% interest	
p13	#50	Caffery	John	defendant				
p13								
p13	#51	Ingram	William	plaintiff	debt appeal	March 1810	cont'd	
p13	#51	Coleman	Joseph	defendant	pay't & issue	Sept 1810	jury/find for pltf $271.70 with 12% interest	
p13							judgment of the county court confirmed	
p13								

MERO DISTRICT SUPERIOR COURT - 1810 - 1813

p13	#52	Whitlow	Coleman	plaintiff	debt appeal	March 1810	cont'd
p13	#52	Coleman	Joseph	defendant	pay/t & issue	Sept 1810	jury/find for pltf $852.29 with 12% interest
p13							judgment of county court confirmed
p14	#53	Harman	Thomas	plaintiff	covenant appeal	March 1810	cont'd
p14	#53	Coleman	Joseph	defendant	dem & joinder	Sept 1810	cont'd
p14						March 1811	cont'd
p14						Sept 1811	cont'd
p14						March 1812	cont'd
p14						Sept 1812	demurrer withdrawn by consent & cont'd
p14						Dec 1812	cont'd
p14						May 1813	jury/find for pltf/damages one cent & costs
p14							
p14	#54	Davidson Academy	President & Trustees	plaintiff	debt appeal	March 1810	cont'd
p14	#54	Coleman	Joseph	defendant	pay/t & issue	Sept 1810	jury/find for pltf $309.60 & 12% interest
p14	#54	Demumbrune	Timothy	defendant			judgment of the county court affirmed
p14							

MERO DISTRICT SUPERIOR COURT   -   1810 - 1813

p14	#55	Cabiness	Charles	plaintiff	case appeal	March 1810	cont'd
p14	#55	Claiborne	Thomas A.	defendant		Sept 1810	cont'd
p14						March 1811	cont'd
p14						Sept 1811	jury/assess pltf damages to $83.53
p14							judg't of the county court aff'd 12%interest
p14							
p14	#56	Harman	Thomas	plaintiff	debt appl	March 1810	cont'd
p14	#56	Claiborne	Thomas A.	defendant	pay/t & issue	Sept 1810	jury/find for pltf $300 debt //damages $50
p14							pltf releases $42.70 part of the debt & damages
p15	#57	Jones	William	plaintiff	debt appeal	March 1810	cont'd
p15	#57	Gordon	John	defendant	pay't & issue	Sept 1810	jury/ find for pltf $100.45 with 12 1/2% interest
p15							
p15	#58	Bell	Henry	plaintiff	debt appeal	March 1810	cont'd
p15	#58	Sommerville	John	defendant	pay/t & issue	Sept 1810	jury/find for pltf $171.81 with 12% interest
p15							
p15	#59	Nusam	Eldridge	plaintiff	case appl	March 1810	cont'd

MERO DISTRICT SUPERIOR COURT - 1810 - 1813

p15	#59	Nichols	John	defendant	non asst/issue	Sept 1810	cont'd
p15						March 1811	cont'd
p15						Sept 1811	jury/find for pltf $119.87
p15							
p15	#60	Murphy	Aexander	plaintiff	original attch't	March 1810	cont'd
p15	#60	Seawell	Benjamin	defendant	appeal	Sept 1810	cont'd
p15						March 1811	cont'd
p15						Sept 1811	cont'd
p15						March 1812	cont'd
p15						Sept 1812	cont'd
p15						Dec 1812	judg/t of the county affirmed with 12% interest
p16	#61	Cabiness	Charles	plaintiff	in error	March 1810	cont'd
p16	#61	Walker	Phillip	plaintiff	errors ass'd	Sept 1810	cont'd
p16	#61	Ralston	Joseph	defendant		March 1811	cont'd
p16						Sept 1811	cont'd

MERO DISTRICT SUPERIOR COURT - 1810 - 1813

							March	
p16							1812	cont'd
p16							Sept	judg't of the county court affirmed with 12%
							1812	interest
p16								
p16	#62	Watkins	Thomas G.	plaintiff	debt appeal		March 1810	cont'd
p16	#62	Sappington	Roger B.	defendant	dem & joinder		Sept 1810	cont'd
p16							March 1811	cont'd
p16							Sept 1811	cont'd
p16							March 1812	cont'd
p16							Sept 1812	defts demurrer overruled/judgment of the county
p16								court affirmed with 12% interest
p16								
p16	#63	Bell	Samuel	plaintiff	debt appeal		March 1810	cont'd
p16	#63	Edmondson	William	defendant	pay't & issue		Sept 1810	jury/find for pltf $319./judgment of the county
p16	#63	Titus	James	defendant				court affirmed with 12% interest
p16								
p16	#64	Lytle	William	plaintiff	debt appeal		March 1810	cont'd
p16	#64	Shute	Thomas	defendant	pay't & issue		Sept 1810	jury/ find for pltf $538.58/judgment of the county

MERO DISTRICT SUPERIOR COURT - 1810 - 1813

p16							court affirmed with 12% interest
p17	#65	Lytle	William	plaintiff	debt appeal	March 1810	cont'd
p17	#65	Shute	Thomas	defendant	pay/t & issue	Sept 1810	jury/ find for pltf $179.94/judgment of the county
p17							court affirmed with 12% interest
p17							
p17	#66	Brewer	Sterling	plaintiff	cov't appeal	March 1810	cont'd
p17	#66	Wade	George	defendant	dem & joinder	Sept 1810	demurrer overruled & writ of enquiry awarded/cont'd
p17					dem overruled	March 1811	cont'd
p17					writ of enquiry	Sept 1811	jury/assess pltfs damages to $504
p17							judgment of the county court affirmed/12% interest
p17							
p17	#67	Winn	Braxton B.	plaintiff	cov't appeal	March 1810	cont'd
p17	#67	Lewis	William T.	defendant	cov't perf'd	Sept 1810	cont'd
p17						March 1811	cont'd
p17						Sept 1811	jury/find for pltf//assess his damages to one cent
p17							judgment for the same & costs
p17							

MERO DISTRICT SUPERIOR COURT - 1810 - 1813

p17	#68	Tait	William	plaintiff	debt appeal	March 1810	cont'd
p17	#68	Brewer	Sterling	adm/deft		Sept 1810	cont'd
p17	#68	Brewer	Allen	deceased		Sept 1811	jury/find for pltf but find deft has no assets in his
p17							hands to be administered/judg for same & costs
p18	#69	Mitchell	John	plaintiff	trespass/appeal	March 1810	cont'd
p18	#69	Nusam	William	defendant	not guilty/issue	Sept 1810	cont'd by consent
p18						March 1811	cont'd
p18						Sept 1811	cont'd
p18						March 1812	jury/find for pltf & assess his damages to $125.00
p18							
p18	#70	Harrison	John	plaintiff	Scifa	March 1810	cont'd
p18	#70	Searcy	Bennet	defts bail		Sept 1810	jury/find Childress hath not paid the costs in the
p18	#70	Childress	Nath'l G.	defendant			writ of Scifa
p18							
p18	#71	Brown	George	plaintiff	covenant	March 1810	cont'd

MERO DISTRICT SUPERIOR COURT - 1810 - 1813

p18	#71	Caffery	John	defendant	cov't performed	Sept 1810	cont'd
p18					special plea	March 1811	defendants death suggested & cont'd
p18						Sept 1811	cont'd
p18						March 1812	defendant being dead this case is abated
p18							
p18	#72	Pate	Willeroy	pltf/adm	Scifa	March 1810	cont'd
p18	#72	Pate	Anthony	deceased		Sept 1810	cont'd
p18	#72	Davis	Anthony & others	defendant		March 1811	cont'd
p18	#72	Blackamore	John [heirs]	deceased		Sept 1811	cont'd
p18						March 1812	cont'd
p18						Sept 1812	cont'd
p18						Dec 1812	discontinued//defendant to pay costs
p19	#73	Frazier	James	plaintiff	debt	March 1810	cont'd
p19	#73	Edmiston	William	defendant	pay't & issue	Sept 1810	dismissed/deft by his atty assumes the costs
p19							

MERO DISTRICT SUPERIOR COURT   -   1810 - 1813

p19	#74	Butler	Thomas R.	plaintiff	debt	March 1810	cont'd
p19	#74	Bradford	William	plaintiff	pay't & issue	Sept 1810	dismissed/deft assumes the costs
	#75	Harris	Arch'd H.	defendant			
p19							
p19	#75	Ingram	Pines	plaintiff	case	March 1810	cont'd
p19	#75	Bedford	John R.	pltf/admr	non asst	Sept 1810	cont'd
p19	#75	Cabiness	Ch.	witness	fully admitted	March 1811	leave granted deft to file an additional plea/cont'd
p19						Sept 1811	cont'd
p19						March 1812	jury/nonsuit/rule to set nonsuit aside/set aside
p19							pltf to pay costs of this term/give additional security
p19						Sept 1812	cont'd
p19						Dec 1812	jury/find for pltf/assess damages to $2191.91
p19							Rule for new trial by deft & cont'd
p19						May 1813	new trial granted/cont'd/deft to pay costs this term &
p19							take depositions of Ch Cabiness
p19							
p19	#76	Baird	John	plaintiff	AB certiorari	March 1810	cont'd

MERO DISTRICT SUPERIOR COURT - 1810 - 1813

p19	#76	Anderson	Patton	defendant	not guilty/issue	Sept 1810	cont'd
p19						March 1811	death of deft suggested//suit abated by death of deft
p20	#77	East	Tarleton	plaintiff	AB certiorari	March 1810	cont'd
p20	#77	Anderson	Patton	defendant	not guilty/issue	Sept 1810	cont'd
p20						March 1811	defts death suggested & cont'd
p20						Sept 1811	abated by defts death
p20							
p20	#78	Goodloe	William & als	pltf/admr	debt certiorari	March 1810	cont'd
p20	#78	Goodloe	Robert	deceased	cov't performed	Sept 1810	cont'd
p20	#78	Ingram	Pines	defendant		March 1811	jury/find for deft $488.57/$438.51 damages
p20							
p20	#79	Mannon	Unity	plaintiff	case/slander	March 1810	cont'd
p20	#79	Elliott	Samuel & wife	defendant	justification	Sept 1810	cont'd
p20						not guilty/issue	March 1811	deft withdraw their plea of not guilty/cont'd
p20							Sept 1811	cont'd

MERO DISTRICT SUPERIOR COURT - 1810 - 1813

p20						March 1812	jury/find for pltf/damages to $500/6% interest
p20							
p20	#80			lessee/pltf	ejectment	March 1810	cont'd
p20	#80	Rutherford	Thomas	owner	ejectment	Sept 1811	cont'd
p20	#80	Wright	William	defendant		March 1811	cont'd
p20						Sept 1811	cont'd by consent
p20						March 1812	dismissed & deft assumes all costs but atty's fee
p21	#81	Sevier	John	pltf/Governor	debt	Sept 1810	cont'd
p21	#81	Searcy	Robert	deft/Treas	condition perf'd	March 1811	cont'd on affidavit of Solicitor Gen'l of 4th Circuit
p21	#81	Jackson	Andrew	deft security	rept & issue	Sept 1811	cont'd by consent
p21	#81	Dickson	William	deft security		March 1812	cont'd
p21						Dec 1812	cont'd on afft of the pltf
p21						May 1813	cont'd -- causes removed
p21							
p21	#82	Flynn	Thomas	plaintiff	covenant	March 1810	cont'd

MERO DISTRICT SUPERIOR COURT - 1810 - 1813

p21	#82	Lewis	William T.	defendant	cov't perf'd	Sept 1810	jury/find for pltf/damages to $631.41
p21							
p21	#83	Williams	Oliver	plaintiff	debt	March 1810	cont'd
p21	#83	Wilson	William	plaintiff	Demr	Sept 1810	cont'd
p21	#83	Norris	Ezekiel	defendant	Enquiry of damg	March 1811	cont'd
p21						Sept 1811	cont'd
p21						March 1812	cont'd
p21						Sept 1812	Demr sustained ...
p21						Dec 1812	jury/assess pltfs damages to $1000
p21							
p21	#84			lessee	ejectment	March 1810	cont'd
p21	#84	Williams	Sampson	owner	not guilty/issue	Sept 1810	cont'd
p21	#84	Johnston	Alexander	defendant		March 1811	cont'd
p21	#84	Hannis	Samuel	defendant		Sept 1811	the death of Alexander Johnston suggested/jury
p21							mistrial by consent
p21						March 1812	cont'd

MERO DISTRICT SUPERIOR COURT - 1810 - 1813

p21						Sept 1812	cont'd
p21						Dec 1812	jury/find for pltf/assess his damages to 1 cent & judg
p22	#85	Den			lessee/pltf	ejectment	March 1810 cont'd
p22	#85	Talbot	Thomas		plaintiff		
p22	#85	McGavock	D.		owner	not guilty/issue	Sept 1810	on the motion of Talbot ordered suit be adjourned to
p22	#85	McNairy	John		defendant		the Circuit Court of Williamson County
p22	#85	Buford	Simeon		defendant		
p22	#85	Wiggin	John P.		defendant		
p22	#85	Byrnes	James		defendant		
p22							
p22	#86	Tait	William		plaintiff	Scifa	March 1810 cont'd
p22	#86	Stuart	Thomas		deft/security	Demurrer	Sept 1810 cont'd
p22	#86	McKean	Joseph		defendant	& joinder	March 1811 cont'd
p22							Sept 1811 cont'd
p22							March 1812 Demurrer overruled & judgment for costs of Scifa
p22							
p22	#87	Wood	Titus		plaintiff	case appeal	March 1810 cont'd

MERO DISTRICT SUPERIOR COURT - 1810 - 1813

p22	#87	Boyd	Richard	defendant	non apt & issue	Sept 1810	cont'd on affdt of pltfs atty
p22	#87	Turner	Joseph	deposition		March 1811	cont'd
p22	#87	Gibbs	Thos.	deposition		Sept 1811	cont't on aff't of deft
p22	#87	Dickinson	Mr.	pltfs atty		March 1812	cont'd
p22						Sept 1812	com. awarded deft to take depositions/cont'd
p22						Dec 1812	cont'd
p22						May 1813	jury/find for pltf/assess his damages to $150 & costs
p22							
p22	#88	Wood	Titus	plaintiff	case/trover appl	March 1810	cont'd
p22	#88	Boyd	Richard	defendant	not guilty/issue	Sept 1810	cont'd on afft of pltfs atty
p22	#88	Turner	Joseph	deposition		March 1811	cont'd
p22	#88	Gibbs	Thos.	deposition		Sept 1811	cont'd on aff't of deft
p22	#88	Dickinson	Mr.	pltfs atty		March 1812	cont'd
p22						Sept 1812	com. awarded deft to take depositions/cont'd
p22						Dec 1812	cont'd

MERO DISTRICT SUPERIOR COURT - 1810 - 1813

p22						May 1813	jury/ find for pltf/assess damages to $149.00 & costs
p23	#89	Bosley	John	plaintiff	debt appl	March 1810	cont'd
p23	#89	Drake	Henry	defendant	no assignment	Sept 1810	cont'd
p23						March 1811	cont'd
p23						Sept 1811	cont'd
p23						March 1812	jury/find for pltf $45.07 & costs
p23							
p23	#90	Lemasters	Isaac	plaintiff	debt appl	March 1810	cont'd
p23	#90	Manifee	James N.	defendant	payment/issue	Sept 1810	cont'd by consent
p23					set off	March 1811	cont'd
p23						Sept 1811	jury/find for pltf debt $525/damages $22.30
p23							judgment of the county court affirmed
p23							
p23	#91	Ivey	Frederick	plaintiff	case appl	March 1810	cont'd
p23	#91	Miller	William	defendant	not guilty/issue	Sept 1810	jury/find deft not guilty/judg for deft for costs
p23							

MERO DISTRICT SUPERIOR COURT - 1810 - 1813

p23	#92	Olive	Abel	plaintiff	debt appl	March 1810	cont'd
p23	#92	Napier	Thomas	defendant	non debit/issue	Sept 1810	jury/find for pltf $150 debt/damages to $9.50
p23							reasons in arrest of judg filed/is by consent adj to
p23							the next Supreme Court of Errors & Appeals
p24	#93	Bustard & Easton		plaintiff	debt appl	March 1810	cont'd
p24	#93	Williams	Lemuel	defendant	payment	Sept 1810	jury/find for pltf $87.86/$3.95 damages
p24					repr & issue		judgment of the county court affirmed
p24							
p24	#94	Rutherford	William	plaintiff	case appl	March 1810	cont'd
p24	#94	Gordon	John	defendant	non asst	Sept 1810	com. for pltf to take deposition of Whitesides/cont'd
p24	#94	Whiteside			set off & issue	March 1811	cont'd
p24						Sept 1811	jury/find for pltf $591.84/12% interest
p24							judgment of the county court affirmed
p24							
p24	#95	Criddle	John	plaintiff	debt appeal	March 1810	cont'd
p24	#95	Perkins	William	defendant	paym't & issue	Sept 1810	jury/find for the pltf $116.50

MERO DISTRICT SUPERIOR COURT - 1810 - 1813

p24							judgment of the county court conf'd
p24							
p24	#96	Eakin	Moses	plaintiff	an appeal	March 1810	cont'd
p24	#96	Easley	William	defendant		Sept 1810	cont'd
p24						March 1811	cont'd
p24						Sept 1811	cont'd
p24						March 1812	cont'd
p24						Sept 1812	cont'd
p24						Dec 1812	jury/find for pltf $33.43
							judgment & bill of exceptions signed & sealed
p25	#97	Connelly	Thomas	plaintiff	case appeal	March 1810	cont'd
p25	#97	Gordon	John	defendant	not guilty/issue	Sept 1810	cont'd
p25						March 1811	cont'd
p25						Sept 1811	jury/find for pltf & assess his damages to $64.80
p25							judgment of the county court affirmed
p25							

MERO DISTRICT SUPERIOR COURT - 1810 - 1813

p25	#98	Kirkman	Thomas	plaintiff	debt appl	March 1810	cont'd
p25	#98	Claiborne	Thomas A.	defendant	payment/issue	Sept 1810	jury/find for pltf $204. debt/damages $13.95
p25					set off		judgment of the county court affirmed
p25							
p25	#99	Rochel	William	plaintiff	debt appeal	March 1810	cont'd
p25	#99	Irvin	John	defendant	pay't & issue	sept 1810	jury/find for pltf/ debt $680. to be discharged by pay't
p25	#99	Hooper	Joseph	defendant			of $361./ judgment of county court confirmed
p25							
p25	#100	Deatheridge	John	plaintiff	case appeal	March 1810	cont'd
p25	#100	Deatheridge	Thomas	plaintiff	non asst/issue	Sept 1810	cont'd
p25	#100	Hardinge	Samuel A.			March 1811	cont'd
p25						Sept 1811	cont'd
p25						March 1812	cont'd
p25						Sept 1812	cont'd
p25						Dec 1812	jury/Mistrial & cont'd
p25						May 1813	jury/Mistrial & cont'd/ cause removed

MERO DISTRICT SUPERIOR COURT - 1810 - 1813

p26	#101	Pinkerton	James & als	plaintiff	petition appeal	March 1810	cont'd
p26	#101	Walker	Peter & wife	defendant	demurrer	Sept 1810	cont'd
p26						March 1811	cont'd
p26						Sept 1811	cont'd
p26						March 1812	cont'd
p26						Sept 1812	cont'd
p26						Dec 1812	cont'd on the aff't of defts agent
p26						May 1813	jury/Nonsuit & judg agst pltf for costs
p26							
p26	#102	Whitfield	Harrison	plaintiff	debt appeal	March 1810	cont'd
p26	#102	Owen	Jabez	defendant	pay't & issue	Sept 1810	jury/find for pltf/ $166.66 debt & $10.75 damages
p26	#102	Owen	Nathan	defendant			judgment of the county court confirmed
p26	#102	Owen	Joshua	defendant			
p26							
p26	#103	Hardiman	Thomas	plaintiff	debt appeal	March 1810	cont'd
p26	#103	Stump	John	defendant	payment/issue	Sept 1810	jury/find for pltf/ $500 debt/damages $23.13

36

MERO DISTRICT SUPERIOR COURT - 1810 - 1813

p26					set off		judgment of the county court affirmed
p26							
p26	#104	Kintzing	Abraham	plaintiff	debt appeal	March 1810	cont'd
p26	#104	Stump	John	defendant	payment/issue	Sept 1810	jury/find for pltf/debt $300/damages $16
p26					set off		judgment of the county court confirmed
p27	#105	Huston	James	plaintiff	debt appeal	March 1810	cont'd
p27	#105	Stump	John	defendant	pay't set off	Sept 1810	jury/find for pltf / debt $81/damages $3.37
p27					issue		judgment of the county court affirmed
p27							rule by deft to set verdict aside/rule for new trial
p27						March 1811	cont'd
p27						Sept 1811	on argument new trial be had at next court
p27						March 1812	cont'd
p27						Sept 1812	cont'd
p27						Dec 1812	jury/ find for pltf/ debt $81/damages $3.37/12% int
p27							judgment of the county court confirmed
p27							
p27	#106	Fleshart	Elizabeth	pltf/admx	debt appl	March 1810	cont'd

MERO DISTRICT SUPERIOR COURT - 1810 - 1813

p27	#106	Fleshart	Francis	deceased	pay't set off	Sept 1810	jury/find for pltf/debt $77.75
p27	#106	Christmas	William	defendant	issue		judgment conf'd agst the principal & securities in
p27							the appeal with 12% int.
p27							
p27	#107	Bustard & Eastin		plaintiff	debt appeal	March 1810	
p27	#107	Searcy	Bennet	defendant	pay't set off &	Sept 1810	jury/ find for pltf $273.42
p27					issue		judgment confirmed/12% interest
p27							
p27	#108	Smith	John	plaintiff	debt appl	March 1810	cont'd
p27	#108	Foster	Anthony	defendant	pay't set off	Sept 1810	jury/ find for pltf $1368.75
p27	#108	Coleman	Joseph	defendant	issue		judgment of the county court confirmed/12% int.
p28	#109	McGavock		plaintiff	caveat appeal	March 1810	cont'd
p28	#109	Ewing		plaintiff		Sept 1810	cont'd
p28	#109	Talbot		plaintiff		March 1811	cont'd
p28	#109	Tait	William	defendant		Sept 1811	cot'd
p28						March 1812	cont'd

MERO DISTRICT SUPERIOR COURT - 1810 - 1813

						Sept	
p28						1812	cont'd
p28						Dec 1812	cont'd
p28						May 1813	jury/ordered the caveat be dismissed & caveators
p28							pay the cost
p28							
p28	#110	Black	John	plaintiff	case trover appl	March 1810	cont'd
p28	#110	Dunn	Michael C.	defendant	not guilty/issue	Sept 1810	cont'd
p28						March 1811	cont'd
p28						Sept 1811	cont'd
p28						March 1812	dismissed/judgment for costs
p28							
p28	#111	Blevins	Henry	plaintiff	scifa	March 1810	cont'd
p28	#111	Williams	Nath'l W.	defts bail		Sept 1810	judgment according to scifa
p28	#111	Mcpherson	John	defendant			
p28							
p28							
p28	#112	Thomas	Richard	plaintiff	scifa	March 1810	judgment according to scifa
p28	#112	Robertson	Elijah [heirs]	defendant			

MERO DISTRICT SUPERIOR COURT - 1810 - 1813

p29	#113	Stump	C. & Co.	plaintiff	case certiorari	March 1810	cont'd
p29	#113	Lovell	James	defendant		Sept 1810	cont'd
p29	#113	Grimes	William	defendant		March 1811	cont'd by consent
p29	#113	Grimes	Philip	deft/exor		Sept 1811	cont'd
p29						March 1812	cont'd
p29						Sept 1812	cont'd
p29						Dec 1812	cont'd
p29						May 1813	death of Wm Grimes suggested/ sci fa to issue
p29							against James Lovell & Philip Grimes exors/cont'd
p29	#114	Watson	James	plaintiff	certiorari	March 1810	cont'd
p29	#114	Murry	John	defendant		Sept 1810	cont'd
p29	#114	Hayes	Robert	defendant		March 1811	cont'd
p29	#114	Harris	Sampson	defendant		Sept 1811	cont'd
p29						March 1812	cont'd

MERO DISTRICT SUPERIOR COURT - 1810 - 1813

p29						Sept 1812	cont'd
p29						Dec 1812	judgment according to scifa
p29							
p29	#115	Allen	John	plaintiff	debt cert.	March 1810	cont'd
p29	#115	Large	Ebenezer	plaintiff		Sept 1810	cont'd
p29	#115	Large	John	plaintiff		March 1811	cont'd
p29	#115	Hinnen	James	defendant		Sept 1811	cont'd
p29						March 1812	cont'd
p29						Sept 1812	on argument ... certiorari dismissed/deft pay costs
p29							
p29	#116	Horton	Josiah	plaintiff	certiorari	March 1810	cont'd
p29	#116	Prince	Francis	defendant		Sept 1810	dismissed by the pltf/deft assume the costs
p30	#117			lessee	ejectment	March 1810	cont'd
p30	#117	McGavock	James	owner	not guilty/issue	Sept 1810	cont'd
p30	#117	Gamble	Edmund			March 1811	cont'd

41

MERO DISTRICT SUPERIOR COURT - 1810 - 1813

p30						Sept 1811	cont'd by consent
p30						March 1812	cont'd by consent
p30						Sept 1812	cont'd
p30						Dec 1812	cont'd
p30						May 1813	dismissed & each party pay their own costs
p30							
p30	#118			lessee	ejectment	March 1810	cont'd
p30	#118	McGavock	James	owner	not guilty/issue	Sept 1810	cont'd
p30	#118	Murry	John	defendant		March 1811	cont'd
p30						Sept 1811	cont'd
p30						March 1812	cont'd
p30						Sept 1812	cont'd
p30						Dec 1812	cont'd
p30						May 1813	jury/find for pltf/assess his damages to one cent
p30							
p30	#119			lessee	ejectment	March 1810	cont'd

MERO DISTRICT SUPERIOR COURT - 1810 - 1813

p30	#119	McGavock	James	owner	not guilty/issue	Sept 1810	cont'd
p30	#119	Birdwell	George	defendant		March 1811	cont'd
p30						Sept 1811	cont'd
p30						March 1812	cont'd
p30						Sept 1812	cont'd
p30						Dec 1812	cont'd
p30						May 1813	jury/Nonsuit/judgment for costs
p30							
p30	#120	Marr	Geo M.	plaintiff	covenant	Sept 1810	cont'd
p30	#120	Bell	George	defendant	writ of enquiry	March 1811	cont'd
p30						Sept 1811	cont'd
p30						March 1812	cont'd
p30						Sept 1812	cont'd
p30						Dec 1812	jury/assess pltfs damages to $82.33 & costs
p31	#121	Robinson	Samuel	plaintiff	debt	Sept 1810	cont'd

MERO DISTRICT SUPERIOR COURT - 1810 - 1813

p31	#121	Harney	Thomas	defendant	decla Dem &	March 1811	cont'd
p31					joinder	Sept 1811	cont'd
p31						March 1812	cont'd
p31						Sept 1812	defts demurrer to pltfs dicta overruled & writ of enquiry
p31							awarded & continued
p31						Dec 1812	jury/ assess the plaintiffs damages to $2000
p31							
p31	#122	Talbot	Thomas	plaintiff	in error	March 1810	cont'd
p31	#122	Bedford	Thomas [heirs]		errors assigned	Sept 1810	cont'd
p31						March 1811	cont'd
p31						Sept 1811	cont'd
p31						March 1812	cont'd
p31						Sept 1812	cont'd
p31						Dec 1812	cont'd
p31						May 1813	by consent ...this cause removed to the next Superior
p31							Court of Errors & Appeals of the 4th Circuit

MERO DISTRICT SUPERIOR COURT - 1810 - 1813

p31							
p31	#123	Farmer	Thomas	plaintiff	debt	Sept 1810	jury/find for pltf/assess damages to $1500/pltf releases
p31	#123	Bradford	Benjamin J.	defendant	rep't & issue		$913.82//judg for $586.18 residue of damages & costs
p31	#123	McCreary	Thomas	defendant			
p31							
p31	#124	Marr	George W. L.	plaintiff	case appl	March 1810	cont'd
p31	#124	Craighead	John B.	defendant	non asst/issue	Sept 1810	cont'd
p31						March 1811	cont'd
p31						Sept 1811	cont'd
p31						March 1812	cont'd
p31						Sept 1812	cont'd
p31						Dec 1812	cont'd
p31						May 1813	jury/find for pltf/assess his damages to $67.25 & costs
p32	#125	Sanderson	Robert	plaintiff	debt appeal	March 1810	cont'd
p32	#125	Overton	Walter H.	defendant		Sept 1810	cont'd

MERO DISTRICT SUPERIOR COURT - 1810 - 1813

p32						March 1811	cont'd
p32						Sept 1811	cont'd
p32						March 1812	cont'd
p32						Sept 1812	cont'd
p32						Dec 1812	jury/Nonsuit/rule to set Nonsuit aside/rule discharged
p32							
p32	#126	Ewing	Alexander	plaintiff	debt appeal	March 1810	cont'd
p32	#126	Lewis	William S.	defendant	payment repn &	Sept 1810	jury/find for pltf $400 debt/ damages $34.66
p32					issue		judgment confirmed
p32							
p32	#127	Folks	Burwell	plaintiff	case appl	March 1810	cont'd
p32	#127	Newnan	John		non asst	Sept 1810	cont'd
p32	#127	Hews	Wm T.	deposition	pay/t & issue	March 1811	cont'd
p32						Sept 1811	cont'd
p32						March 1812	cont'd
p32						Sept 1812	cont'd

MERO DISTRICT SUPERIOR COURT - 1810 - 1813

p32						Dec 1812	cont'd by consent/Com' to take depo
p32						May 1813	jury/find for deft & assess damages to $103 & costs
p32							rule for new trial/new trial granted & cont'd
p32							Cause removed
p32							
p32	#128	Salter	Michael	plaintiff	debt appeal	March 1810	cont'd
p32	#128	Stump	Christopher	defendant	pay't set off	Sept 1810	jury/ find for pltf $479.94/judg of county court conf'd
p32					issue		pltf by his attorney releases the debt & damages
p33	#129	Childress	John, Jr	plaintiff	debt appeal	March 1810	cont'd
p33	#129	Stump	John	defendant	payment	Sept 1810	cont'd
p33					set off & issue	March 1811	cont'd
p33						Sept 1811	jury/ find debt $800/damages $9.60
p33							
p33	#130	Napier	Richard C.	plaintiff	debt appeal	March 1810	cont'd
p33	#130	Waggaman	Thomas E.	defendant	pay't set off & issue	Sept 1810	jury/ find for pltf $146.61/damages $19.42 judgment confirmed
p33							
p33							

MERO DISTRICT SUPERIOR COURT - 1810 - 1813

p33	#131	Smith	Robert	plaintiff	coven't appeal	March 1810	cont'd
p33	#131	Hudson	Thomas	defendant	special plea	Sept 1810	cont'd
p33					paym't in part	March 1811	dismissed by pltf/deft assumes the costs
p33							
p33	#132	Puckett	Edward	plaintiff	debt appeal	March 1810	cont'd
p33	#132	Young	John L.	defendant		Sept 1810	cont'd
p33	#132	McGavock	David	referee		March 1811	cont'd by consent/ referred to McGavock & Cooper &
p33	#132	Cooper	Edmund	referee			whomever they choose & decision to be made judgment of the court
p33							
p33						Sept 1811	cont'd
p33						March 1812	cont'd
p33						Sept 1812	cont'd
p33						Dec 1812	jury/find for pltf $4.79 & costs
p34	#133	Cain	Daniel & wife	plaintiff	AB appl	March 1810	cont'd
p34	#133	Metcalf	Jlai	defendant	not guilty/issue	Sept 1810	Cont'd

48

MERO DISTRICT SUPERIOR COURT - 1810 - 1813

p34						March 1811	cont'd
p34						Sept 1811	cont'd
p34						March 1812	cont'd
p34						Sept 1812	cont'd
p34						Dec 1812	jury/ find for pltf/ damages to $10
p34							
p34	#134	Williamson	John S.	plaintiff	debt appl	March 1810	cont'd
p34	#134	Sommerville	John	defendant	pay/t set off issue	Sept 1810	jury/find for pltf/ $203.98/ judg't of county court conf'd
p34							
p34							
p34	#135	Lytle	Archibald	plaintiff	Scifa appl	March 1810	cont'd
p34	#135	Claiborne	Thomas A.	defts bail	pay't & issue	Sept 1810	jury/ find for pltf/judg't according to Scifa
p34	#135	Catlett	Hanson	deft			judgment of the county court confirmed
p34							
p34	#136	Marr	George W. L.	plaintiff	Scifa appl	March 1810	cont'd
p34	#136	Claiborne	Thomas A.	defts bail	pay't & issue	Sept 1810	jury/find for pltf/judg't of county court confirmed
p34	#136	Catlett	Hanson	defendant			

MERO DISTRICT SUPERIOR COURT - 1810 - 1813

p35	#137	Stapleton	George	plaintiff	case appl	March 1810	cont'd
p35	#137	Claiborne	Thomas A.	defendant	non asst/issue	Sept 1810	cont'd
p35					issue	March 1811	cont'd
p35						Sept 1811	cont'd
p35						March 1812	cont'd
p35						Sept 1812	cont'd
p35						Dec 1812	jury/find for plty & assess his damages to $397
p35							pltf releases $63.88/deft acquitted & discharged
p35							judgment of the county court affirmed
p35							
p35	#138	Ingram	Henry	plaintiff	debt appl	March 1810	cont'd
p35	#138	Claiborne	Thomas A.		pay't set off	Sept 1810	jury/ find for pltf $489.58/damages $25.11
p35					issue		judgment of the county court confirmed
p35							
p35	#139	Ellis	Joseph T.	pltf/admr	debt appl	March 1810	cont'd
p35	#139	Mullen	Mary	pltf/admx		Sept 1810	jury/find for pltf bal. of debt/$35.19 damages
p35	#139	Mullen	William S.	deceased			judgment confirmed

MERO DISTRICT SUPERIOR COURT - 1810 - 1813

p35	#139	Gordon	John	defendant			
p35							
p35	#140	Lyle	George	plaintiff	debt appl	March 1810	cont'd
p35	#140	Gordon	John	defendant	pay't set off	Sept 1810	jury/ find for pltf $600/damages #36.50
p35					issues		judgment confirmed
p36	#141	Nelson	John	plaintiff	debt appl	March 1810	cont'd
p36	#141	Gordon	John	defendant		Sept 1810	cont'd
p36						March 1811	cont'd
p36						Sept 1811	cont'd
p36						March 1812	cont'd
p36						Sept 1812	cont'd
p36						Dec 1812	jury/find for pltf $1.50/judg't of county court confirmed
p36							
p36	#142	Kirkman	Thomas	plaintiff	debt appl	March 1810	cont'd
p36	#142	Edmondson	Robert	defendant	pay't/issue	Sept 1810	jury/find for pltf $85.90 debt/damages $5.66
p36							judg't of the county court confirmed
p36							

MERO DISTRICT SUPERIOR COURT - 1810 - 1813

p36	#143	May	Francis	plaintiff	debt appeal	March 1810	cont'd
p36	#143	Roper	William	defendant	pay't set off	Sept 1810	jury/find for pltf $90.50 debt/damages $4.64
p36					issue		
p36							
p36	#144	Elliston	Joseph T.	plaintiff	debt appeal	March 1810	cont'd
p36	#144	Edmondson	William	defendant	pay't set off	Sept 1810	jury/ find for pltf $199.50 residue of debt/damgs $26.23
p36	#144	Ramsey	Thomas	defendant	issue		judgment confirmed
p37	#145	Barnes	James, Jr	plaintiff	case appeal	March 1810	cont'd
p37	#145	Rains	John, Jr.	defendant	not guilty/issue	Sept 1810	cont'd
p37					justification	March 1810	cont'd
p37					special plea	Sept 1811	cont'd
p37						March 1812	dismissed by pltfs atty & deft assumes the costs
p37							
p37	#146	Nusam	William	plaintiff	case appeal	March 1810	cont'd
p37	#146	Nichols	John	defendant	non asst/issue	Sept 1810	cont'd
p37						March 1811	cont'd

MERO DISTRICT SUPERIOR COURT - 1810 - 1813

p37						Sept 1811	cont'd
p37						March 1812	cont'd
p37						Sept 1812	dismissed by pltfs atty & each party pay own costs
p37							
p37	#147	Donelson	John	plaintiff	Scifa	March 1810	cont'd
p37	#147	Stuart	Thomas	defts bail	payment	Sept 1810	cont'd
p37	#147	Den	John	lessee		March 1811	judgment according to Scifa
p37	#147	Bedford	Thomas	owner			
p37							
p37	#148	Metcalf	John	plaintiff	case certiorari	March 1810	motion to dismiss certiorari/cont'd
p37	#148	Gordon	John	defendant	non asst/issue	Sept 1810	cont'd
p37						March 1811	cont'd
p37						Sept 1811	cont'd
p37						March 1812	cont'd
p37						Sept 1812	cont'd
p37						Dec 1812	cont'd

MERO DISTRICT SUPERIOR COURT - 1810 - 1813

p37						May 1813	jury/find for pltf & assess damages to $176.27& costs
p38	#149	Lytle	William, Jr.	plaintiff	case certiorari	March 1810	cont'd
p38	#149	Shute	Thomas	defendant	dicta, Dem &	Sept 1810	cont'd
p38					joinder	March 1811	cont'd
p38						Sept 1811	cont'd
p38						March 1812	cont'd
p38						Sept 1812	certiorari dismissed & deft to pay the costs
p38							
p38	#150	Lofton	William	plaintiff	covenant	March 1810	cont'd
p38	#150	Christmas	William	defendant	cov't performed	Sept 1810	cont'd
p38						March 1811	cont'd
p38						Sept 1811	dismissed & deft by his attorney assumes the costs
p38							
p38	#151	Long	Richard H.	plaintiff	petition for	March 1810	cont'd
p38	#151	Long	John Joseph & others	defendant	division of land	Sept 1810	cont'd

MERO DISTRICT SUPERIOR COURT - 1810 - 1813

p38						March 1811 cont'd
p38						Sept 1811 cont'd
p38						March 1812 cont'd
p38						Sept 1812 cont;d
p38						Dec 1812 cont'd
p38						May 1813 cont'd cause removed see No 7
p38						
p38	#152	Den	John	pltf/lessee	ejectment	March 1810 cont'd
p38	#152	Cummins	David & others	owner	not guilty/issue	Sept 1810 cont'd
p38	#152	Tatum	Howel	defendant		March 1811 cont'd
						Sept 1811 dismissed by the pltfs atty/judgment
p39	#153	Boyd	Richard	plaintiff	in error	March 1810 cont'd
p39	#153	Davidson Academy	President & Trustees	defendant	errors assigned	Sept 1810 cont'd
p39						March 1811 cont'd
p39						March 1810 cont'd

MERO DISTRICT SUPERIOR COURT - 1810 - 1813

p39						March 1812	cont'd
p39						Sept 1812	judgment of the county court confirmed
p39							
p39	#154	Perkins	Nicholas T.	plaintiff	debt	March 1810	cont'd
p39	#154	Gilliam	Edy	deft/extrx	cov't performed	Sept 1810	cont'd
p39	#154	Gilliam	Divirix	deceased		March 1811	cont'd
p39						Sept 1811	cont'd/ defts death suggested/Scifa to his executrix
p39						March 1812	cont'd/ ordered this suit be rev. agst Edy Gilliam,extx
p39						Sept 1812	cont'd
p39						Dec 1812	cont'd
p39						May 1813	jury/find for pltf/assess damages to $1100 & costs
p39							
p39	#155	York	William	plaintiff	debt	Sept 1810	cont'd
p39	#155	Irwin	John	defendant		March 1811	cont'd
p39						Sept 1811	pltf called/Nonsuited/ judg. for costs
p39							

MERO DISTRICT SUPERIOR COURT - 1810 - 1813

p39	#156	Washington	Elizabeth	pltf/admx	detinue	March 1810 cont'd
p39	#156	Washington	Gray	deceased	non detinue &	Sept 1810 cont'd
p39	#156	Washington	Thomas	defendant	issue	March 1811 cont'd
p39						Sept 1811 cont'd
p39						March 1812 cont'd
p39						Sept 1812 cont'd
p39						Dec 1812 cont'd on affd of pltfs atty
p39						May 1813 jury/find for defendant/judg't agst pltf for costs
p39						rule for new trial/new trial granted/pltf pay costs/cont'd
p39						Cause removed/ See #8
p40	#157	Lacy	Hopkins	plaintiff	debt	Sept 1810 cont'd
p40	#157	Robertson	Sarah	deft/extx		March 1811 cont'd
p40	#157	Robertson	James	deft/extr		Sept 1812 Nonsuit & judgment for costs
p40	#157	Searcy	Robert	deft/extr		
p40	#157	Searcy	Bennet	deft/extr		
p40						

MERO DISTRICT SUPERIOR COURT - 1810 - 1813

p40	#158	Sevier	John Esqr/Governor	plaintiff	debt	Sept 1810	cont'd
p40	#158	Searcy	Robert [late treas/Mero]	defendant		March 1811	cont'd
p40	#158	Jackson	Andrew	defts bail		Sept 1811	cont'd
p40	#158	Williams	Sampson			March 1812	cont'd
p40						Sept 1812	cont'd
p40						Dec 1812	cont'd
p40						May 1813	cont'd/Cause removed
p40							
p40	#159	Anderson	William P.	plaintiff	case	March 1810	cont'd
p40	#159	Gilbert	William	defendant	not guilty & issue	Sept 1810	cont'd for dicta
p40	#159	Hyde	Henry	defts bail		March 1811	cont'd
p40	#159	Hickman	Thos.			Sept 1811	
p40						March 1812	
p40						Sept 1812	
p40						Dec 1812	Nonsuit/judgment
p40							

58

MERO DISTRICT SUPERIOR COURT - 1810 - 1813

p40	#160			lessee	ejectment	March 1810	dismissed by the lessee of the pltf
p40	#160	Ewing	Alexander	owner			
p40	#160	German	Shaderick	defendant			
p40	#160	German	Robert	defendant			
p41	#161	Evans	Robert	plaintiff	case	March 1810	cont'd
p41	#161	Nusem	Francis	defendant		Sept 1810	cont'd
p41						March 1811	cont'd
p41						Sept 1811	cont'd
p41						March 1812	cont'd
p41						Sept 1812	cont'd
p41						Dec 1812	cont'd
p41						May 1813	jury/find for pltf/assess his damages to one cent
p41							
p41	#162	Jackson	James	plaintiff	debt appeal	Sept 1810	cont'd
p41	#162	Jackson	Washington	plaintiff	pay't & issue	March 1811	jury/find for pltf/balance of debt $342.74/damgs $20.12
p41	#162	Reeves	Robert C.	defendant			judgment of the county court affirmed
p41							

MERO DISTRICT SUPERIOR COURT - 1810 - 1813

p41	#163	Ogden	Benjamin	plaintiff	debt appeal	Sept 1810	jury/find for pltf $163 debt/damages $8.71
p41	#163	Brunson	John	plaintiff	set off issues		judgment of the county court confirmed
p41	#163	Searcy	Bennet	defendant			
p41							
p41	#164	Nelson	John	plaintiff	case appl	Sept 1810	cont'd
p41	#164	Gordon	John	defendant	not guilty	March 1811	cont'd
p41					justification/issue	Sept 1811	Com. awarded the pltf to take deposition
p41						March 1812	cont'd
p41						Sept 1812	cont'd
p41						Dec 1812	Jury/find for pltf/assess his damages to $150
p42	#165	Waggamand	Thomas E.	plaintiff	case appl	Sept 1810	cont'd by consent
p42	#165	Sulivan	Clemen	plaintiff	non asst/issues	March 1811	cont'd
p42	#165	Erwin	Joseph	defendant	set off	Seept 1811	cont'd
p42						March 1812	cont'd
p42						Sept 1812	cont'd

MERO DISTRICT SUPERIOR COURT - 1810 - 1813

p42						Dec 1812	cont'd
p42						May 1813	jury/find for pltf/asses his damages to $381.11
p42							judgment of the county court affirmed
p42							cause remanded to the Circuit Court
p42							
p42	#166	Talbot	Thomas	pltf/exor	debt appl	Sept 1810	jury/find for pltfs $214.03
p42	#166	McGavock	David	pltf/exor	pay/t & rep'r		judgment of the county court affirmed
p42	#166	Weakley	Robt	pltf/exor	issues		
p42	#166	Talbot	Matthew	deceased			
p42	#166	Barrow	Willie	defendant			
p42							
p42	#167	Talbot	Thomas	pltf/exor	debt appeal	Sept 1810	jury/find for pltf $150.90
p42	#167	McGavock	David	pltf/exor	pay't rep'n issues		judgment of the county court affirmed
p42	#167	Weakley	Robt	pltf/exor			
p42	#167	Talbot	Matthew	deceased			
p42	#167	Barrow	Willie	defendant			
p42							
p42	#168	Moseley	Jacob	plaintiff	covenant appl	Sept 1810	cont'd
p42	#168	Ferguson	William	defendant	demurrer	March 1811	
p42						Sept 1811	the defendant dismisses his appl
p42							judgment of the county affirmed

MERO DISTRICT SUPERIOR COURT - 1810 - 1813

p43	#169	Tate	Alexander	plaintiff	case appeal	Sept 1810	cont'd
p43	#169	Erwin	Joseph	defendant	non asst issue	March 1811	cont'd
p43						Sept 1811	cont'd
p43						March 1812	cont'd
p43						Sept 1812	cont'd
p43						Dec 1812	dismissed at the defendants certs. Judg't
p43							
p43	#170	Anderson	Nathaniel S.	plaintiff	debt appeal	Sept 1810	Jury/find for pltf $100 bal of debt/$12.23 damages
p43	#170	Mullin	William	defendant	pay't & issue		judg't of the county court confirmed
p43							
p43	#171	Edwards	Gray	plaintiff	AB appl	Sept 1810	cont'd
p43	#171	Scales	Henry	next friend	not guilty/issue	March 1811	
p43	#171	Rutherford	Thomas	defendant	Son assault ...?	Sept 1811	
p43						March 1812	
p43						Sept 1812	

MERO DISTRICT SUPERIOR COURT   -   1810 - 1813

p43						Dec 1812	jury/find for pltf & assess his damages to $73.75
p43							
p43	#172	Waggaman	Thomas E.	plaintiff	debt appl	Sept 1810	jury/find for pltf/bal. of debt $78/damages $6.60
p43	#172	Gordon	John	defendant	pay't set off		
p43					issue		
p44	#173	Talbot	Thomas	plaintiff	debt appeal	Sept 1810	jury/find for pltf $84.25 & $73.05 damages
p44	#173	Gordon	John	defendant			judg't of county court affirmed
p44							
p44	#174	Anderson	John	plaintiff	debt appl	Sept 1810	jury/find for pltf $381.80 & $17.17 damages
p44	#174	Gordon	John	defendant	pay't set off		judgment of the county court affirmed
p44					issues		
p44							
p44	#175	Purvis	Allen	plaintiff	debt appeal	Sept 1810	jury/find for pltf/ debt $196.25 & damages $36.58
p44	#175	Gordon	Allen	defendant			judgment of the county court confirmed
p44							
p44	#176	Porter	Thomas & Co.	plaintiff	case appeal	Sept 1810	cont'd
p44	#176	Gordon	John	defendant	paym't set off	March 1811	cont'd
p44					issues	Sept 1811	cont'd
p44						March 1812	cont'd

MERO DISTRICT SUPERIOR COURT - 1810 - 1813

p44						Sept 1812	cont'd
p44						Dec 1812	jury/find for pltf/damages of $110.00
p44							judgment of the county court affirmed
p45	#177	Richardson	Alexander	plaintiff	debt appl	Sept 1810	jury/find for pltf $393.35 debt & damages
p45	#177	Searcy	Bennet	defendant	pay't set off		judgment of the county court confirmed
p45					issues		
p45							
p45	#178	Richardson	Alexander	plaintiff	debt appl	Sept 1810	jury/ find for pltf $56.40 debt & damages
p45	#178	Searcy	Bennet	defendant	payment set off		judgment of the county court confirmed
p45					issues		
p45							
p45	#179	Anderson	John	plaintiff	debt appeal	Sept 1810	jury/find for pltf $1032.33 debt/damages $41.50
p45	#179	Coleman	Joseph	defendant	payment set off		judgment of the county court confirmed
p45					issues		
p45							
p45	#180	Cockrell	John, Junr	plaintiff	debt appl	Sept 1810	jury/ find for pltf $903. debt/damages $66.82
p45	#180	Coleman	Joseph	defendant	payment set off		judgment of the county court confirmed
p45	#180	McNairy	Nath'l	defendant	issues		
p46	#181	Williams	Littlebury	pltf/exor	debt appeal	Sept 1810	jury/find for pltf/ debt $525./damages $25.81

MERO DISTRICT SUPERIOR COURT - 1810 - 1813

p46	#181	Williams	John	deceased	payment set off		judgment of the county court confirmed
p46	#181	Wyche	Nathaniel	defendant	issues		
p46							
p46	#182	Wilks	Joseph	plaintiff	debt appeal	Sept 1810	cont'd
p46	#182	Cooper	Edmond	defendant		March 1811	cont'd
p46						Sept 1811	cont'd
p46						March 1812	cont'd
p46						Sept 1812	cont'd
p46						Dec 1812	jury/Nonsuit/judgment for costs
p46							
p46	#183	Casey	Randolph	plaintiff	debt appl	Sept 1810	cont'd
p46	#183	Deatheridge	John	defendant		March 1811	cont'd
p46						Sept 1811	cont'd
p46						March 1812	cont'd
p46						Sept 1812	cont'd
p46						Dec 1812	jury/find for defendant/rule by pltf for new trial/cont'd

MERO DISTRICT SUPERIOR COURT - 1810 - 1813

p46						May 1813	on agreement ordered rule for a new trial be discharged
p46							
p46	#184	Barfield	Frederick	plaintiff	debt appeal	Sept 1810	cont'd
p46	#184	Lynch	James	defendant	payment set off	March 1811	
p46					issues	Sept 1811	jury/ find for pltf $244.50 interest $32.79/judg conf'd
p47	#185	Richardson	Alexander	plaintiff	debt appl	Sept 1810	jury/find for pltf $520.89 bal. of debt & damgs
p47	#185	Phillips	John	defendant	payment set off		judgment of the county court confirmed
p47					issues		
p47							
p47	#186	McNairy	Nathaniel A.	plaintiff	debt appl	Sept 1810	dismissed by the pltf & deft assumes the costs
p47	#186	Hughs	Robert	defendant	payment set off		
p47					issues		
p47							
p47	#187	Ryland	Thomas	plaintiff	debt appl	Sept 1810	judg for amount of the repl. bond with interest & costs
p47	#187	Ingram	Pines	defendant			
p47	#187	Ingram	William	defendant			
p47	#187	Cabiness	Charles	defendant			
p47							
p47	#188	Jackson	Andrew	plaintiff	debt appl	Sept 1810	cont'd

MERO DISTRICT SUPERIOR COURT - 1810 - 1813

p47	#188	Hutchings	John	plaintiff		March 1811	dismissed by the pltfs & defts pay costs
p47	#188	Pryer	Sam'l	defendant			
p47	#188	Lewis	William T.	defendant			
p47	#188	Hall	Charles M.	defendant			
p48	#189	Metcalf	Jlai	plaintiff	case appeal	Sept 1810	cont'd
p48	#189	Waggaman	Thomas E.	defendant	non asst & issues	March 1811	cont'd
p48						Sept 1811	dismissed & deft assumes the costs
p48							
p48	#190	Smith	John H. & Co.	plaintiff	case appeal	Sept 1810	cont'd
p48	#190	Poyzer	George	defendant	demurrer	March 1811	cont'd
p48					writ of enquiry	Sept 1811	cont'd
p48						March 1812	cont'd
p48						Sept 1812	Demurrer overruled & writ of enquiry awarded/cont'd
p48						Dec 1812	cont'd
p48						May 1813	judgment for $340 by consent
p48							

MERO DISTRICT SUPERIOR COURT - 1810 - 1813

p48	#191	Porter	Ambrose	plaintiff	debt appeal	Sept 1810	jury/find for pltf debt $137.50/damages $12.50
p48	#191	Nichols	John	defendant			judgment of the county court confirmed
p48							
p48	#192	Childress	John, Jr	plaintiff	debt appl	Sept 1810	cont'd
p48	#192	Stump	John	defendant		March 1811	
p48						Sept 1811	jury/ find for pltf debt $480 & damages $68.32
p48							judgment of the county court confirmed
p49	#193	Park	Joseph	plaintiff	debt appeal	Sept 1810	jury/find for pltf $166.28 debt/damgs $16.45
p49	#193	Goodrich	John	defendant	pay't set off		judgment of the county court affirmed
p49					issues		
p49							
p49	#194	Fuller	Nehemiah	plaintiff	debt appl	Sept 1810	jury/find for pltf $119. debt/damages $10.71
p49	#194	Erwin	Joseph	defendant	pay't set off		judgment with 10% int. on amt of judgment in the county court
p49					issues		
p49							
p49	#195	Bowles	John	plaintiff	debt appl	Sept 1810	jury/find for pltf $106 debt damages $9.54
p49	#195	Erwin	Joseph	defendant	payment set off		judgment of the county court affirmed
p49					issues		
p49							

MERO DISTRICT SUPERIOR COURT - 1810 - 1813

p49	#196	Robertson	Duncan	plaintiff	debt appl	Sept 1810	jury/find for pltf $280 debt/damgs $18.20
p49	#196	Stump	John	defendant	pay't set off		judgment of the county court affirmed
p49					issues		
p50	#197	Green	Elisha	plaintiff	Debt appl	Sept 1810	jury/find for pltf $100 debt $6.17 damages
p50	#197	Erwin	John	defendant	pay't set off		judgment of the county court affirmed
p50					rep'n & issues		
p50							
p50	#198	Waggaman	Thomas E.	plaintiff	case appl	Sept 1810	cont'd by consent
p50	#198	Erwin	Joseph	defendant	payment & issue	March 1811	cont'd
p50					set off	Sept 1811	cont'd
p50						March 1812	cont'd
p50						Sept 1812	cont'd
p50						Dec 1812	cont'd
p50						May 1813	jury/find for pltf & assess his damages to $2615.52
p50							judgment of the county court confirmed
p50							
p50	#199	Waggaman	Thomas E.	plaintiff	covenant appl	Sept 1810	cont'd by consent

MERO DISTRICT SUPERIOR COURT - 1810 - 1813

p50	#199	Erwin	Joseph	defendant	demr & joinder	March 1811	cont'd
p50						Sept 1811	cont'd
p50						March 1812	cont'd
p50						Sept 1812	demurrer overruled & enquiry of dam. awarded/cont'd
p50						Dec 1812	cont'd
p50						May 1813	jury/assess pltfs damages to $884.85 & costs
p50							damages released by pltfs atty, 6 months docket
p50							
p50	#200	Waggaman	Thomas E.	plaintiff	case appl	May 1812	cont'd by consent/com. awarded deft to take depositions
p50	#200	Erwin	Joseph	defendant	not guilty & issue	March 1811	cont'd
p50	#200	Billings	Wm	deposition		Sept 1811	
p50	#200	Carron	Charles L.	deposition		March 1812	
p50	#200	Wright	Abraham	deposition		Sept 1812	
p50						Dec 1812	
p50						May 1813	jury/find for pltf & assess damages to $1745.59 & costs
p50							judgment of the county court affirmed

MERO DISTRICT SUPERIOR COURT - 1810 - 1813

p51	#201	Whittle	Fortescue	plaintiff	debt appl	Sept 1810	jury/find for pltf $655.44/judg of county court confirmed
p51	#201	Bedford	John R.	defendant	pay't & issue		By consent the verdict & judgment set aside & new trial
p51						March 1811	cont'd
p51						Sept 1811	jury/find for the pltf $655.44/judg't for 12 1/2% int.
p51							
p51	#202	Hudnell	Ezekiel	plaintiff	debt appl	Sept 1810	cont'd
p51	#202	Balance	Joshua	defendant		March 1811	cont'd
p51	#202	Davis	John	defendant		Sept 1811	cont'd
p51						March 1812	cont'd
p51						Sept 1812	cont'd
p51						Dec 1812	judg't of the county court affirmed
p51							
p51	#203	Jackson	James	plaintiff	debt appl	Sept 1810	jury/find for pltf balance of debt $93.45/dam. $5.90
p51	#203	Jackson	Wash'n	plaintiff	payment/set off		judgment of the county court affirmed
p51	#203	Patterson	Thomas	defendant	issue		
p51							

MERO DISTRICT SUPERIOR COURT - 1810 - 1813

p51	#204	Hyde	Mary	plaintiff	debt appl	Sept 1810	cont'd on aff't of deft/com to take depositions
p51	#204	Lesslie?	William	defendant	payment set off	March 1811	cont'd
p51	#204	Williamson	Benjamin	defendant	issues	Sept 1811	jury/find for pltf/ debt $76.00/damages $4.90
							affirmed with 12% interest
p52	#205	Shelby	David	plaintiff	petition	Sept 1810	motion by pltf to dismiss appl/ cont'd
p52	#205	Stump	C.	plaintiff	ferry appl	March 1811	cont'd
p52	#205	Nichols	John & others	defendant		Sept 1811	cont'd
						March 1812	cont'd
						Sept 1812	cont'd
						Dec 1812	cont'd
						May 1813	cont'd/ Cause removed
p52							
p52	#206	Monroe	David P.	plaintiff	covenant appl	Sept 1810	cont'd
p52	#206	Beaty	William	plaintiff	demr & joinder	March 1811	cont'd
p52	#206	Lewis	William T.	defendant		Sept 1811	cont'd

MERO DISTRICT SUPERIOR COURT - 1810 - 1813

						March	
p52						1812	cont'd
p52						Sept 1812	pltf demurrer to defts pleas sustained
p52							inquiry of damages awarded/cont'd
p52						Dec 1812	jury/assess pltfs damages to $1713.03
p52							Bill of exceptions filed/writ of error granted
p52							pltf releases $113.03/judg't of county court affirmed
p52							
p52	#207	Weakley	Robert	plaintiff	covenant appl	Sept 1810	cont'd
p52	#207	Coleman	Joseph	defendant	dem. & joinder	March 1811	cont'd
p52					cov't perf'd	Sept 1811	cont'd
p52					issue	March 1812	cont'd
p52						Sept 1812	pltfs demurrer to defts plea sustained/plea overruled/cont'd
p52						Dec 1812	Jury/find for pltf & assess damages to one cent/judg't
p52							
p52	#208	McGinissey	John	plaintiff	case appl	Sept 1810	cont'd
p52	#208	Stewart	Peter B.	deft/admr		March 1811	jury/dismissed by pltf/judgment for costs
p52	#208	Stewart	William	deceased			

MERO DISTRICT SUPERIOR COURT - 1810 - 1813

p53	#209	Anderson	John	plaintiff	in error	Sept 1810	cont'd
p53	#209	Lytle	William	plaintiff	errors assigned	March 1811	cont'd
p53	#209	Mullen	Jonah	plaintiff		Sept 1811	cont'd
p53	#209	Scott	Samuel	defendant		March 1812	cont'd
p53						Sept 1812	judg't of the county court reversed
p53							
p53	#210	Doak	John	plaintiff	petition for divorce	Sept 1810	order for als subpoena & cont'd
p53	#210	Doak	Susanna	defendant		March 1811	als spa not found, order for pltfs spa to issue
p53						Sept 1811	cont'd
p53						March 1812	dismissed by the petitioner in proper person
p53							judg't that petitioner pay the costs of the petition
p53							
p53	#211	Chanis	James	plaintiff	debt cert.	Sept 1810	motionby pltf to dismiss the cert't cont'd
p53	#211	Bryant	Shaderick	defendant		March 1811	cont'd
p53						Sept 1811	

MERO DISTRICT SUPERIOR COURT - 1810 - 1813

p53						March 1812	
p53						Sept 1812	motion to dismiss the cert't overruled/ cont'd
p53						Dec 1812	jury/Nonsuit & judg't for costs
p53							
p53	#212	Hodge	Francis	plaintiff	debt certiorari	Sept 1810	cont'd
p53	#212	Dillon	Thomas		rep't & issue	March 1811	cont'd
p53					dem'r & joinder	Sept 1811	cont'd
p53						March 1812	cont'd
p53						Sept 1812	motion to set aside the order of the county court
p53							quashing the cert./ overruled/ motion by deft to dismiss
p53							Certiorari dismissed & judg't pltf pay the costs
p53							Writ of error granted
p54	#213	Anderson	Patton	plaintiff	in error	Sept 1810	motion by deft in error to quash the writ of error/cont'd
p54	#213	Drake	John	plaintiff	errors assigned	March 1811	cont'd
p54	#213	Searcy	Bennet	plaintiff		Sept 1811	cont'd

MERO DISTRICT SUPERIOR COURT - 1810 - 1813

p54	#213	Sample	John & Co.	defendant		March 1812	cont'd
p54						Sept 1812	the death of Patton Anderson suggested
p54							judgment affirmed
p54							
p54	#214	Richardson	Alexander	plaintiff	in error	Sept 1810	cont'd
p54	#214	Mathews	James	defendant	errors assigned	March 1811	cont'd
p54						Sept 1811	cont'd
p54						March 1812	cont'd
p54						Sept 1812	judgment of the county court reversed/judg't for costs
p54							
p54	#215	King	James	plaintiff	debt certiorari	Sept 1810	death of James King suggested/motion by pltf to dismiss
p54	#215	Caison	Charles S.	plaintiff			cont'd
p54	#215	Hamilton	James	defendant		March 1811	cont'd
p54	#215	McLendon	Dennis	defendant		Sept 1811	cont'd
p54						March 1812	ordered that the certiorari be dismissed/...deft pay costs
p54							
p54	#216	Crosky	George D.	plaintiff	debt certiorari	Sept 1810	motion by pltf to dismiss cert./cont'd

MERO DISTRICT SUPERIOR COURT - 1810 - 1813

p54	#216	Hamilton	James	defendant		March 1811 cont'd
p54	#216	McLendon	Dennis	defendant		Sept 1811 cont'd
p54						March 1812 ordered that the certiorari be dismissed.../deft pay costs
p55	#217	Davis	John	plaintiff	Scifa appl	Sept 1810 cont'd
p55	#217	Deaderick	George M.	defendant	pay't & issue	March 1811 cont'd
p55						Sept 1811 cont'd
p55						March 1811 cont'd
p55						Sept 1812 cont'd
p55						Dec 1812 jury/ say deft hath not paid the debt in the Scifa
p55						May 1813 judg't there is such record/judg't of county court conf'd
p55						
p55	#218	Elam	Robert	plaintiff	debt appl	Sept 1810 cont'd
p55	#218	Owen	Rich'd B.	defendant		March 1811 cont'd
p55						Sept 1811 cont'd
p55						March 1812 cont'd

MERO DISTRICT SUPERIOR COURT   -   1810 - 1813

p55						Sept 1812	cont'd
p55						Dec 1812	jury/ find for pltf $23.00/judg't of county court aff'd
p55							rule by deft for a new trial/cont'd
p55						May 1813	new trial granted/ cont'd/
p55							Cause removed/ see #156
p55							
p55	#219	McClung	Hugh	plaintiff	debt appl	Sept 1810	jury/find for deft $1000/damages $60.83
p55	#219	Hickman	Thomas	defendant	pay't set off		judgment of the county court affirmed
p55	#219	Sappington	Roger B.	defendant	issue		
p55							
p55	#220	Gregory	Edmond	plaintiff	divorce petition	Sept 1810	issue on alias supoena/order for publication
p55	#220	Gregory	Polly	defendant		March 1811	als not found/cont'd
p55						Sept 1811	proclamation & cont'd
p55						March 1812	cont'd
p55						Sept 1812	cont'd
p55						Dec 1812	cont'd
p55						May 1813	cont'd
p55							Cause removed - See #11

MERO DISTRICT SUPERIOR COURT - 1810 - 1813

p56	#221	Metcalf	Ilai	plaintiff	case appl	Sept 1810	cont'd
p56	#221	Whiteside	Jinken	defendant	non asst issue	March 1811	cont'd
p56					set off	Sept 1811	cont'd
p56						March 1812	cont'd
p56						Sept 1812	cont'd
p56						Dec 1812	cont'd by consent
p56						May 1813	cont'd on affdt of defendant/cause removed/ see #12
p56							
p56	#222	Jackson	Jas.	plaintiff	debt appl	Sept 1810	cont'd
p56	#222	Jackson	Wash.	plaintiff	pay't & issue	March 1811	cont'd
p56	#222	Bell	Hugh	deft/admr	adm't & issue	Sept 1811	jury/find for pltf $111.81/damages $14.24
p56	#222	Nelson	Robert	deceased			judgment aff'd
p56							
p56	#223	Sebastian	Isaac	plaintiff	case appl	Sept 1810	cont'd
p56	#223	Payne	Matthew	defendant	non asst/issue	March 1811	cont'd

MERO DISTRICT SUPERIOR COURT - 1810 - 1813

p56						Sept 1811	cont'd
p56						March 1812	cont'd
p56						Sept 1812	cont'd
p56						Dec 1812	jury/find for pltf $178.00/judg of county court aff'd
p56							writ of error granted deft/bond & security given
p56							
p56	#224	Deaderick & Sommerville		plaintiff	debt appl	Sept 1810	jury/find for pltf debt $221.95/damages $9.95
p56	#224	Scruggs	Finch	defendant	payment set off		judgment of the county court aff'd
p56					issue		
p57	#225	Claiborne	Thomas A.	plaintiff	debt appl	Sept 1810	jury/find for pltf/debt $100/damages $4.50
p57	#225	Newnan	John	defendant	pay't set off		judgment of the county court aff'd
p57					issues		
p57							
p57	#226	Claiborne	Thomas A.	plaintiff	debt appl	Sept 1810	cont'd
p57	#226	Newnan	John	defendant	Dem'r & joinder	March 1811	cont'd
p57						Sept 1811	cont'd
p57						March 1812	cont'd

MERO DISTRICT SUPERIOR COURT - 1810 - 1813

p57						Sept 1812	Demurrer overruled/judg't of the county court affirmed
p57							
p57	#227	Neilson	David	plaintiff	debt appl	Sept 1810	jury/ find for pltf/ debt $450/damages $55.50
p57	#227	Erwin	Joseph	defendant	pay't set off		judgment of the county court affirmed
p57					issues		
p57							
p57	#228	Graves	William	plaintiff	caveat appeal	Sept 1810	cont'd
p57	#228	Resse?	Gustaves	defendant		March 1811	cont'd by consent
p57						Sept 1811	cont'd
p57						March 1812	dismissed by the pltf/deft assumes the costs
p58	#229	Sugg	Jonah	plaintiff	case appl	Sept 1810	cont'd
p58	#229	Demoss	Abraham	defendant	not guilty & issue	March 1811	cont'd
p58					additional pleas	Sept 1811	cont'd by consent/deft to take depositions in NC
p58						March 1812	cont'd
p58						Sept 1812	cont'd
p58						Dec 1812	additional plea filed/cont'd

MERO DISTRICT SUPERIOR COURT - 1810 - 1813

p58						May 1813	cont'd Cause removed - see #13
p58							
p58	#230	Shelby	David	plaintiff	petition for road	Sept 1810	motion by pltfs to dismiss the appl/cont'd
p58	#230	Stump	C.	plaintiff	& ferry appl	March 1811	cont'd
p58	#230	McNairy	John	defendant		Sept 1811	cont'd
p58						March 1812	cont'd
p58						Sept 1812	cont'd
p58						Dec 1812	cont'd
p58						May 1813	the appellant dismisses his appeal & Stump to pay costs
p58							
p58	#231	Deaderick & Sommerville		plaintiff	case appl	Sept 1810	cont'd
p58	#231	Joslin	Benjamin	defendant	non asst & issue	March 1811	cont'd
p58	#231	Hall	E. S.	mediator		Sept 1811	by consent referred to mediators/award to be det't of court
p58	#231	Buchanan	John	mediator			award determined that deft pay pltf $59.33 & costs
p58	#231	Thompson	Robt	mediator			
p58							

MERO DISTRICT SUPERIOR COURT - 1810 - 1813

p58	#232	May	Francis	plaintiff	case appl	Sept 1810	cont'd
p58	#232	Stephens	Robert	defendant	not guilty / issues	March 1811	cont'd
p58						Sept 1811	cont'd
p58						March 1812	cont'd
p58						Sept 1812	cont'd
p58						Dec 1812	Nonsuit / judgment for costs
p59	#233	Boggs	James	plaintiff	covenant appl	Sept 1810	cont'd
p59	#233	Davidson	Nathan	plaintiff	dem & joinder	March 1811	cont'd
p59	#233	Hudson	Thomas	defendant		Sept 1811	cont'd
p59						March 1812	cont'd
p59						Sept 1812	Demurrer overruled & Writ of Enquiry awarded/cont'd
p59						Dec 1812	jury/assess pltfs damages to $1386.32
p59							judgment of the county court affirmed
p59							
p59	#234	Terry	William	plaintiff	case appl	Sept 1810	cont'd

MERO DISTRICT SUPERIOR COURT - 1810 - 1813

p59	#234	Terry	Susannah	pltf/admx	non asst/issue	March 1811	cont'd	
p59	#234	Clay	John W.	defendant		Sept 1811	cont'd	
p59						March 1812	cont'd	
p59						Sept 1812	death of pltf suggested & cont'd	
p59						May 1813	suit recived in name of Susannah Terry, admx/cont'd	
p59							Cause removed - see #14	
p59								
p59	#235	Jackson & Hutchings		plaintiff	appeal	Sept 1810	cont'd	
p59	#235	Pryor	Samuel	defendant		March 1811	death of Sam'l Pryor suggested/dismissed by pltfs atty
p59	#235	Hall	Charles M.	defendant			defendants pay costs	
p59	#235	Lewis	William T.	defendant				
p59								
p59	#236	Gordon	John	plaintiff	case appl	Sept 1810	cont'd	
p59	#236	Downs	James P.	defendant	non asst set off	March 1811	cont'd	
p59					issues	Sept 1811	cont'd	
p59						March 1812	cont'd	
p59						Sept 1812	cont'd	

MERO DISTRICT SUPERIOR COURT   -   1810 - 1813

p59						Dec 1812	cont'd
p59						May 1813	cont'd
p60	#237	Caldwell	William	plaintiff	certiorari	Sept 1810	motion by pltf to dismiss cert./cont'd
p60	#237	Lewis	William T.	defendant		March 1811	cont'd
p60						Sept 1811	cont'd
p60						March 1812	cont'd
p60						Sept 1812	cont'd
p60						Dec 1812	Nonsuit/judg't for costs
p60							
p60	#238	Johnston	Isaac	plaintiff	Scifa	Sept 1810	plea pay't & special plea & issues
p60	#238	McCarty	John	defendant		March 1811	cont'd
p60	#238	Cage	Reuben	shff bail		Sept 1811	cont'd
p60						March 1812	cont'd
p60						Sept 1812	cont'd
p60						Dec 1812	Nonsuit/judgment for costs

MERO DISTRICT SUPERIOR COURT   -   1810 - 1813

p60							
p60	#239	Claiborne	Thomas A.	plaintiff	In error	Sept 1810	cont'd
p60	#239	Newnan	John	defendant	errors assigned	March 1811	cont'd
p60					joinder	Sept 1811	cont'd
p60						March 1812	cont'd
p60						Sept 1812	judg't of the county court affirmed
p60							
p60	#240	Cartwright	James	plaintiff	case	Sept 1810	cont'd for dicta
p60	#240	Cartwright	Thomas	deft/exor	Dem'r & joinder	March 1811	cont'd
p60	#240	Cartwright	Jacob	deft/exor	Dem'r withdrawn	Sept 1811	
p60	#240	Cartwright	David	deft/exor	Non asst & issue	March 1812	
p60	#240	Cartwright	Robert	deceased		Sept 1812	
p60	#240	Grundy	Felix	pltfs bail		Dec 1812	
						May 1813	Demurrer withdrawn by consent/cont'd
							Cause removed See #16

MERO DISTRICT SUPERIOR COURT - 1810 - 1813

p61	#241	Eakin	Moses	plaintiff	case	Sept 1810	cont'd
p61	#241	Lyon	Henry	defendant	non asst/issues	March 1811	cont'd
p61	#241	Tyree	Richardson	pltfs bail		Sept 1811	cont'd
p61	#241	Shelby	Anthony B.	defts bail		March 1812	cont'd
p61						Sept 1812	cont'd
p61						Dec 1812	jury/ Mistrial/cont'd
p61						May 1813	cont'd of affd't of pltf Cause removed See #17
p61							
p61	#242	Fausset	Richard	plaintiff	debt	Sept 1810	Dicta/plea payment/no assignment/cont'd
p61	#242	Buford	Simpson	defendant	payment	March 1811	cont'd
p61	#242	Overton	John	pltfs bail	repl/issues	Sept 1811	cont'd
p61	#242	Metcalf	Ilai	defts bail		March 1812	cont'd
p61	#242	McCutcheon	Thos.	defts bail		Sept 1812	cont'd
p61						Dec 1812	deft withdraws his pleas/judg for debt $100/int. $18.10
p61							
p61	#243	Sumner	Joseph	plaintiff	case	Sept 1810	dismissed by pltf/deft assumes the costs

MERO DISTRICT SUPERIOR COURT - 1810 - 1813

p61	#243	Dawns	James P.	defendant				
p61	#243	Grundy	Felix	pltfs bail				
p61	#243	Probart	Wm L.	defts bail				
p61	#243	Porter	Thos	defts bail				
p61								
p61	#244			lessee	ejectment	Sept 1810	John White to landlord & Wm Roberts under the common
p61	#244	Mayfield	John	owner	not guilty & issue		rule plead not guilty & issue/cont'd
p61	#244	Roberts	William	defendant		March 1811	cont'd
p61	#244	White	John	defendant		Sept 1811	cont'd
p61	#244	Waller	Thos	pltfs bail		March 1812	cont'd
p61	#244	Nelson	Thos	defts bail		Sept 1812	cont'd
p61	#244	Seawell	Thomas	defts bail		Dec 1812	Nonsuit/judgment for costs
p62	#245			lessee	ejectment	Sept 1810	Wm Parker landlord & Isaac Curry tenant enter into common
p62	#245	Mayfield	John	owner/pltf	not guilty/issue		rule & plead not guilty
p62	#245	Curry	Isaac	defendant		March 1811	cont'd
p62	#245	Parker	Wm	deft/owner		Sept 1811	dismissed by the pltfs atty/deft assumes the costs
p62	#245	Waller	Thos	pltfs bond			
p62	#245	Curry	R. B.	defts bond			
p62								

88

MERO DISTRICT SUPERIOR COURT - 1810 - 1813

p62	#246	Barnes	James, Junr	plaintiff	case	Sept 1810	cont'd
p62	#246	Rains	John, Junr	defendant		March 1811	cont'd
p62	#246	Barnes	James, Senr	pltfs bail		Sept 1811	deft surrenders himself in discharge of his bail
p62	#246	Williams	L.	defts bail		March 1812	dismissed by pltfs atty & deft assumes the costs
p62	#246	Robertson	Christopher	defts bail			
p62	#246	Rains	Wm	defts bail			
p62	#246	Tait	Wm	defts bail			
p62							
p62	#247	Baker	Isaac	plaintiff	case	Sept 1810	dicta filed
p62	#247	Thomas	Jesse W.	defendant	demurrer/joinder	March 1811	cont'd
p62	#247	Searcy	Bennet	pltfs bail		Sept 1811	cont'd
p62	#247	Haggatt	John	defts bail		March 1812	cont'd
p62						Sept 1812	cont'd
p62						Dec 1812	Demurrer overruled & Eng of damages awarded/cont'd
p62						May 1813	jury/assess pltfs damages to $420.63 & costs
p62							
p62	#248	White	Thomas	plaintiff	case	Sept 1810	cont'd

MERO DISTRICT SUPERIOR COURT - 1810 - 1813

p62	#248	Hudson	Westley	defendant	not guilty/issue	March 1811	cont'd
p62	#248	Stump	John	pltfs bail		Sept 1811	plea not guilty & issue/cont'd
p62	#248	Criddle	John	defts bail		March 1812	cont'd
p62	#248	Douglas	Henry	defts bail		Sept 1812	cont'd
p62						Dec 1812	cont'd
p62						May 1813	jury/find for pltf/assess damages to $59 & costs
p63	#249	White	John	plaintiff	debt	Sept 1810	judgment by default/find debt of $600/int from 1 Jan 1810
p63	#249	Bell	Samuel	defendant			
p63	#249	Phillips	Joseph	pltfs bail			
p63							
p63	#250	Williams	Sam'l W.	pltf/admr	debt	Sept 1810	cont'd
p63	#250	Fox	Paulina F.	pltf/admx	payment/issue	March 1811	cont'd
p63	#250	Fox	Thomas	deceased		Sept 1811	jury/ find for pltf/ debt $134.50/damages $19.75
p63	#250	Harney	Thomas	defendant			
p63	#250	Balch	Alfred	pltfs bail			
p63	#250	Durkenson	Jacob	defts bail			
p63	#250	Walker	Matthew P.	defts bail			
p63							

MERO DISTRICT SUPERIOR COURT - 1810 - 1813

p63	#251	Earthman	Sarah [an infant]		case	Sept 1810	cont'd
p63	#251	Earthman	Isaac [next friend]	plaintiff		March 1811	dismissed by the pltfs atty/defts assume the costs
p63	#251	Merriman	William & wife	defendant			
p63	#251	Earthman	Isaac	pltfs bail			
p63	#251	Criddle	John	defts bail			
p63	#251	Cox	John S.	defts bail			
p63							
p63	#252	Jordan	James	plaintiff	case	Sept 1810	cont'd
p63	#252	Ross	Daniel	defendant	not guilty & issue	March 1811	cont'd
p63	#252	Jourdan	Meredith	pltfs bail		Sept 1811	cont'd
p63	#252	Turner	William	defts bail		March 1812	cont'd
p63	#252	Chumbley	Joseph	defts bail		Sept 1812	cont'd
						Dec 1812	jury/Nonsuit/judgment for costs
p64	#253	Tennison	Samuel	plaintiff	debt	Sept 1810	plea condition performed
p64	#253	Robertson	Christopher	defendant	condition perf'd	March 1811	cont'd
p64	#253	Green	Benj.	pltfs bail	rep'n & issue	Sept 1811	jury/find for pltf/damages $100/judgment
p64	#253	Perkins	Philip	defts bail			

MERO DISTRICT SUPERIOR COURT   -   1810 - 1813

p64	#253	Wade	George	defts bail			
p64							
p64	#254	Hess	William	plaintiff	case	Sept 1810	discontinued/judgment for costs
p64	#254	McAlister	Thomas	defendant			
p64							
p64	#255	Jackson	Henry	plaintiff	debt	Sept 1810	plea payment ...
p64	#255	Harney	Thomas	defendant	pay't/rep'n/issue	March 1811	cont'd
p64	#255	Barry	R. D.	pltfs bail		Sept 1811	jury/find for pltf $200/damages $22
p64	#255	Phillips	Wm	defts bail			
p64	#255	Beck	John	defts bail			
p64	#255	Allen	Drury M.	defts bail			
p64							
p64	#256	Hickman	Thomas	plaintiff	case	Sept 1810	cont'd
p64	#256	Dixon	William	defendant		March 1811	cont'd
p64	#256	Parker	Jess	pltfs bail		Sept 1811	cont'd
p64	#256	Rice	Joel	defts bail		March 1812	cont'd
p64	#256	Nichols	David	defts bail		Sept 1812	cont'd
p64						Dec 1812	cont'd

MERO DISTRICT SUPERIOR COURT - 1810 - 1813

p64					May 1813	dismissed by pltf/judg for pltf for remainint costs
p65	#257	Overton	John	pltf/exor	debt	Sept 1810 cont'd
p65	#257	Mulheron	James	pltf/exor	demurrer	March 1811 cont'd
p65	#257	Ewing	Andrew	pltf/exor	demurrer withdrn	Sept 1811 deft withdraws his demurrer & pleads payment & issue
p65	#257	Molloy	Thomas	deceased	pay't & issue	March 1812 cont'd
p65	#257	Horton	Jonah	defendant		Sept 1812 cont'd
p65	#257	Ewing	Nathan	pltfs bail		Dec 1812 cont'd on affdvt of deft/take depositions
p65	#257	Hilton	Dan'l	deposition		May 1813 jury/Mistrial/cont'd
p65						cause removed/see #18
p65	#258	Baker	Isaac	plaintiff	debt	Sept 1810 plea payment & issue
p65	#258	Easten	Thomas	defendant	pay't & issue	March 1811 cont'd
p65	#258	Searcy	Bennet	pltfs bail		Sept 1811 jury/find for pltf/ debt $252.75/damages $18.95
p65						
p65	#259	Seawell	Benjamin	plaintiff	case	Sept 1810 discontinued/judgment for costs
p65	#259	Dunn	Michael C.	defendant		
p65						

MERO DISTRICT SUPERIOR COURT - 1810 - 1813

p65	#260	Heard	James	plaintiff	covt.	Sept 1810	judgment of default & writ of enquiry awarded
p65	#260	O'Bannon	P. N. [use of]		enquiry awarded	March 1811	cont'd
p65	#260	Anderson	Patton	defendant		Sept 1811	cont'd
p65	#260	Hayes	O. B.	pltfs bail		March 1812	cont'd
p65	#260	Anderson	William P.	Exor.		Sept 1812	cont'd
p65						Dec 1812	the deft death suggested/Scifa to exor
p66	#261	Tennisson	Samuel	plaintiff	AB	Sept 1810	Decla issues
p66	#261	Demoss	John	defendant	not guilty	March 1811	cont'd
p66	#261	Thompson	Jacob	pltfs bail	justification/issue	Sept 1811	cont'd by consent
p66	#261	Demoss	Lewis	defts bail		March 1812	Cont'd
p66						Sept 1812	cont'd
p66						Dec 1812	dismissed by the pltf/deft assumes the costs
p66							
p66	#262	Porter	Alexander	plaintiff	case	Sept 1810	decla
p66	#262	Bell	Montgomery	defendant	decla non asst	March 1811	cont'd

94

MERO DISTRICT SUPERIOR COURT - 1810 - 1813

p66	#262	Smith	Wm	pltfs bail	issue	Sept 1811	cont'd
p66						March 1812	cont'd
p66						Sept 1812	cont'd
p66						Dec 1812	jury/find for pltf/assess his damages to $144.50
p66							
p66	#263	Marr	John	plaintiff	covt., Decla	Sept 1810	decla
p66	#263	Lewis	Charles G.	plaintiff	Dem & joinder	March 1811	cont'd
p66	#263	Napier	Thomas	defendant		Sept 1811	cont'd
p66	#263	Hayes	O. B.	pltfs bail		March 1812	cont'd
p66						Sept 1812	cont'd
p66						Dec 1812	defendant withdraws his Dem./confesses judg. for $165.65
p66							
p66							
p66	#264	Beasley	Jesse	plaintiff	Scifa	Sept 1810	als Scifa to Wilson County/cont'd
p66	#264	Armstrong	Martin [heirs of]	defendant		March 1811	[made known to Jos. W. Anderson; Ux & others not found]
p66	#264	Armstrong	Jos. W.				cont'd

MERO DISTRICT SUPERIOR COURT - 1810 - 1813

p66							Sept 1811	Scifa to issue
p66							March 1812	cont'd
p66							Sept 1812	judgment according to Scifa
p67	#265	Corothers	Thomas	plaintiff	case		Sept 1810	issue alias
p67	#265	Lytle	William, Senr	defendant			March 1811	cont'd
p67	#265	Bradford	Thos. G.	pltfs bail			Sept 1811	cont'd
p67	#265	Childress	John, Jr.	defts bail			March 1812	cont'd
p67	#265	Anderson	Wm P.	defts bail			Sept 1812	cont'd
p67							Dec 1812	Nonsuit/judgment for costs
p67								
p67	#266	Corothers	James	plaintiff	case		Sept 1810	issue alias
p67	#266	Lytle	William, Senr	defendant			March 1811	cont'd
p67	#266	Bradford	Thos. G.	pltfs bail			Sept 1811	cont'd
p67	#266	Anderson	Wm P.	defts bail			March 1812	cont'd
p67	#266	Childress	John, Jr.	defts bail			Sept 1812	cont'd

MERO DISTRICT SUPERIOR COURT - 1810 - 1813

p67						Dec 1812	Nonsuit/judgment for costs
p67							
p67	#267	Hooker	Elizabeth	plaintiff	cov't	Sept 1810	cont'd
p67	#267	Hooker	Nathan	plaintiff	covenant perf'd	March 1811	
p67	#267	Hooker	Ann [wife of Nathan]	plaintiff	Demurrer	Sept 1811	
p67	#267	Burt	Christopher	plaintiff		March 1812	death of deft suggested/Scifa to Green & Dyer
p67	#267	Christmas	William	defendant		Sept 1812	cont'd
p67	#267	Grundy	F.	pltfs bail		Dec 1812	Demurrer withdrawn/cont'd
p67	#267	Lewis	Wm T.	defts bail		May 1813	cont'd Cause removed see #19
p67	#267	Allen	David	defts bail			
p67	#267	Green	Sherwood	exor			
p67	#267	Dyer	Joel	exor			
p67							
p67	#268	Allen	Samuel	plaintiff	case	Sept 1810	cont'd
p67	#268	Lesuere	Littlebury	plaintiff		March 1811	
p67	#268	Williamson	John S.	defendant		Sept 1811	dismissed by pltf/deft assumes payment of his own atty
p67	#268	Grundy	Felix	pltfs bail			
p67	#268	Bradford	Thos.	defts bail			

MERO DISTRICT SUPERIOR COURT - 1810 - 1813

p68	#269	Perry	George	plaintiff	debt	Sept 1810	cont'd
p68	#269	Compton	Richard	defendant	rep'n & issue	March 1811	cont'd
p68	#269	Grundy	Felix	pltfs bail	payment/issue	Sept 1811	cont'd
p68	#269	Hodge	James	defts bail		March 1812	dismissed by pltf/judgment for costs
p68							
p68	#270	Kennedy & Calhoon		plaintiff	debt	Sept 1810	cont'd
p68	#270	Foster	Anthony	defendant	payment/issue	March 1811	cont'd
p68						Sept 1811	cont'd
p68						March 1812	cont'd
p68						Sept 1812	cont'd
p68						Dec 1812	jury/find for pltf/$2000 debt/damages $954.50
p68							
p68	#271	Goodloe	John M.	plaintiff	debt	March 1811	cont'd
p68	#271	Lewis	William T.	defendant		Sept 1811	
p68	#271	Dickinson	John	pltfs bail		March 1812	

98

MERO DISTRICT SUPERIOR COURT - 1810 - 1813

p68						Sept 1812	judgment by default/ debt $98/damages 17.99
p68							judgment by default set aside/deft allowed to plead/cont'd
p68						Dec 1812	jury/find for pltf/ debt $98/damages $25.50
p68							
p68	#272	Tipton	Edward	plaintiff	petition for divorce	March 1811	Scifa not found/cont'd
p68	#272	Tipton	Rebecca	defendant		Sept 1811	cont'd
p68	#272	Palmer	Martin	pltfs bail		March 1812	order for publication in the 'Examiner' in Nashville 4 weeks
p68	#272	Lovell	James	pltfs bail		Sept 1812	cont'd
p68						Dec 1812	cont;d
p68						May 1813	cont'd Cause removed see #20
p69	#273	Thomas	Jesse W.	plaintiff	case appl	March 1811	cont'd
p69	#273	Thomas	Mary	deft/exrx	non asst set off	Sept 1811	
p69	#273	Thomas	Phinihas	deceased	issue	March 1812	
p69	#273	Scruggs	Finch	deft/exor.		Sept 1812	
p69	#273	Thomas	Jesse	deceased		Dec 1812	Com. awarded pltf to take deposition/jury/find for pltf

MERO DISTRICT SUPERIOR COURT - 1810 - 1813

p69	#273	Gray	Joseph	deposition			$662.87/Rule for a new trial/cont'd
p69						May 1813	Rule for new trial discharged/judgment of the county court
p69							affirmed
p69							
p69	#274	Goodloe	John M.	plaintiff	case appl	March 1811	cont'd
p69	#274	Claiborne	Thomas A.	defendant	non asst pay't	Sept 1811	cont'd
p69					set off & issue	March 1812	cont'd
p69						Sept 1812	cont'd
p69						Dec 1812	jury/ find for pltf & assess damages of $636.02
p69							judgment of the county court affirmed/writ of error granted
p69							
p69	#275	Crutcher	Thomas	plaintiff	debt appl	March 1811	cont'd
p69	#275	Demoss	Lewis	defendant	payment/issue	Sept 1811	jury/ find for pltf/ debt $500 & damages $33.94
p69							
p69	#276	Mullen	Josiah	plaintiff	case appl	March 1811	cont'd
p69	#276	Whiteside	Jinken	defendant	non asst/issue	Sept 1811	cont'd
p69						March 1812	cont'd

MERO DISTRICT SUPERIOR COURT - 1810 - 1813

p69						Sept 1812	cont'd
p69						Dec 1812	cont'd
p69						May 1813	dismissed & deft assumes the costs
p70	#277	Dabney	John	plaintiff	on a caveat	March 1811	cont'd
p70	#277	Sappington	Roger B.	defendant	appl	Sept 1811	cont't
p70						March 1812	cont't
p70						Sept 1812	cont't
p70						Dec 1812	jury/ find the issues of fact/cont'd
p70						May 1813	adjourned by consent to the next Court of Errors & Appeals
p70							for the 4th circuit
p70							
p70	#278	Shaw	Terrence	plaintiff	debt cer.	March 1811	cont'd
p70	#278	Craighead	Thomas B.	defendant		Sept 1811	cont'd
p70						March 1812	cont'd
p70						Sept 1812	cont'd

MERO DISTRICT SUPERIOR COURT - 1810 - 1813

p70						Dec 1812	cont'd
p70						May 1813	jury/ Nonsuit/judg't for costs
p70							
p70	#279	Davidson Academy	President & Trustees	plaintiff	debt appl	March 1811	cont'd
p70	#279	Horton	Josiah	defendant	payment/issue	Sept 1811	jury/ find for pltf $326.05
p70							
p70	#280	Page	Absolom	plaintiff	debt appl	March 1811	cont'd
p70	#280	Brooks	Matthew, Jr.	defendant		Sept 1811	cont'd
p70						March 1812	judgment confessed by the deft for $6.80
p71	#281	Wright	Elizabeth	pltf/admx	debt appl	March 1811	cont'd
p71	#281	Wright	John	deceased	payment set off	Sept 1811	jury/ find for pltf $125.17 debt/ $6.25 damages
p71	#281	Gordon	John	defendant	issue		
p71							
p71	#282	Tait	William	plaintiff	In error	March 1811	cont'd
p71	#282	Poyzer	George	defendant	errors assigned	Sept 1811	cont'd
p71						March 1812	cont'd

102

MERO DISTRICT SUPERIOR COURT - 1810 - 1813

p71						Sept 1812	cont'd
p71						Dec 1812	judgment of the county court affirmed/ by consent the
p71							judgment is set aside/cont'd
p71						May 1813	cont'd cause removed see #21
p71							
p71	#283	Bustard & Eastin		plaintiff	case appl	March 1811	cont'd
p71	#283	McCreary	Nathaniel	defendant	non asst set off issues	Sept 1811	dismissed by pltfs atty/judgment for costs
p71							
p71							
p71	#284	Hall	Elihu & Co.	plaintiff	case appl	March 1811	cont'd
p71	#284	Watson	Thomas	defendant	non asst/issues	Sept 1811	cont'd
p71						March 1812	cont'd
p71						Sept 1812	cont'd
p71						Dec 1812	cont'd
p71						May 1813	jury/ find for pltf / $1240./judgment of co ct affirmed
p72	#285	Flint	John	plaintiff	Scifa appl	March 1811	cont'd

MERO DISTRICT SUPERIOR COURT - 1810 - 1813

p72	#285	Johnson	Exum	defts bail	pay't	Sept 1811	cont'd
p72	#285	Saltor	Michael	defendant	surrender	March 1812	cont'd
p72						Sept 1812	cont'd
p72						Dec 1812	cont'd
p72						May 1813	jury/ find for pltf/judgment of the county affirmed
p72							
p72	#286	Dowling	Harris	plaintiff	appl	March 1811	cont'd
p72	#286	Hickman	Thomas	defendant	not guilty/issue	Sept 1811	cont'd
p72						March 1812	cont'd
p72						Sept 1812	cont'd
p72						Dec 1812	cont'd
p72						May 1813	Demurrer sustained/deft to pay costs/cont'd
p72							cause removed see #22
p72							
p72	#287	McGavock	David	plaintiff	In error	March 1811	cont'd
p72	#287	Ward	Joseph	defendant	errors assigned	Sept 1811	cont'd

104

MERO DISTRICT SUPERIOR COURT - 1810 - 1813

p72	#287	Paxton	Isaac	defendant		March 1812	cont'd
p72						Sept 1812	cont'd
p72						Dec 1812	cont'd
p72						May 1813	Paxtons death suggested/judg't of county court affirmed
p72							
p72	#288	Wright	Elizabeth	pltf/admx	case appl	March 1811	cont'd
p72	#288	Wright	John	deceased	non asst/issues	Sept 1811	cont'd
p72	#268	Bell	Montgomery	defendant		March 1812	cont'd
p72						Sept 1812	cont'd
p72						Dec 1812	cont'd
p72						May 1813	cont'd on afft of the deft/ cause removed See #23
p73	#289	Roberts	Thomas	plaintiff	case appl	March 1811	cont'd
p73	#289	Porter	Thomas	defendant	not guilty/issue	Sept 1811	cont'd
p73						March 1812	dismissed by the pltf/judgment for costs
p73							

MERO DISTRICT SUPERIOR COURT - 1810 - 1813

p73	#290	Slade	Jeremiah	plaintiff	debt appl	March 1811	cont'd
p73	#290	Anderson	William P.	defendant	conditions perf'd	Sept 1811	
p73					rep'n & issue	March 1812	
p73						Sept 1812	
p73						Dec 1812	
p73						May 1813	jury/find in favor of deft/judgment of the county court aff'd
p73							
p73	#291	Seawell	Benjamin, Senr	plaintiff	case	March 1811	adjourned to the Circuit Court of Wilson Co. on petition
p73	#291	Quinn	Michael C.	defendant	justification/issue		and affidavit of the pltf
p73	#291	Edmondson	Robt	pltfs bail			
p73							
p73	#292	Spickard	Jacob	plaintiff	Scifa	March 1811	Scifa dismissed
p73	#292	Trice	John	defendant			
p73	#292	Bradshaw	William	defts bail			
p74	#293	Beard	Zebuland	plaintiff	Scifa	March 1811	dismissed
p74	#293	Bradshaw	William	debts bail			
p74	#293	Trice	John	defendant			
p74							

MERO DISTRICT SUPERIOR COURT - 1810 - 1813

p74	#294	Edwards	Thomas, Senr	plaintiff	Scifa	March 1811	judgment according to scifa
p74	#294	Edwards	Adonejah	plaintiff			
p74	#294	Edwards	Thomas, Junr	plaintiff			
p74	#294	Hale	James	plaintiff			
p74	#294	Donahoe	John	defts bail			
p74	#294	Barnes	Thomas	defendant			
p74							
p74	#295	Nichols	John	plaintiff	ejectment appl	March 1811	dismissed by D. M. McGavock the appellant
p74	#295	McGavock	David	defendant	not guilty/issue		judgment of the county court affirmed
p74							
p74	#296	Thurmon	John	plaintiff	debt	March 1811	cont'd
p74	#296	Roper	William	defendant		Sept 1811	dismissed/deft assumes the costs
p74	#296	Henry	John	pltfs bail			
p74	#296	Josten	Benj.	defts bail			
p75	#297	Huckeby	John	plaintiff	case	March 1811	plea - payment & issue
p75	#297	Coleman	Joseph	defendant	payment/issue	Sept 1811	cont'd
p75	#297	Murphy	Wm	pltfs bail		March 1812	cont'd
p75						Sept 1812	cont'd
p75						Dec 1812	cont'd

MERO DISTRICT SUPERIOR COURT - 1810 - 1813

p75						May 1813	jury/verdict for pltf for $133.50
p75							
p75	#298	Davis	Obed	plaintiff	AB	March 1811	dismissed by the pltfs atty/deft assumes the costs
p75	#298	Merriman	Wm	defendant			
p75	#298	Earthman	James	pltfs bail			
p75	#298	Lencar	Buchanan	pltfs bail			
p75							
p75	#299	Gray	Jacob	plaintiff	case	March 1811	cont'd
p75	#299	Erwin	Joseph	defendant		Sept 1811	cont'd
p75	#299	Dickenson	Jno.	pltfs bail		March 1812	cont'd
p75	#299	Craighead	John B.	defts bail		Sept 1812	Commission awarded pltf to take deposition/2 days notice
p75	#299	Coxe	Thos	deposition		Dec 1812	cont'd
p75	#299	Donnally	John	deposition		May 1813	Commission for pltf to take deposition/ 12 hours notice
p75	#299	Benton	Jesse	deposition			Cause removed see #157
p75							
p75	#300	Erwin	Joseph	plaintiff	case	March 1811	cont'd
p75	#300	Gray	Jacob	defendant		Sept 1811	cont'd
p75	#300	Grundy	F.	pltfs bail		March 1812	cont'd

MERO DISTRICT SUPERIOR COURT - 1810 - 1813

p75	#300	Anderson	William P.	defts bail		Sept 1812	cont'd
p75	#300	Roper	Rich'd	defts bail		Dec 1812	cont'd
						May 1813	Nonsuit/judgment for costs
p76	#301	Simpson	Sally	pltf/admx	case	March 1811	plead non asst & issue
p76	#301	Manifee	Jonas	pltf/admr	non asst & issue	Sept 1811	cont'd
p76	#301	Billings	William	defendant		March 1812	cont'd
p76	#301	Grundy	F.	pltfs bail		Sept 1812	cont'd
p76	#301	Erwin	Joseph	defts bail		Dec 1812	cont'd
p76	#301	Craighead	Jno. B.	defts bail		May 1813	jury/find for pltf/ $207.94 & costs
p76							
p76	#302	Hunt	John W.	plaintiff	case	March 1811	cont'd
p76	#302	Carson	Charles S.	defendant		Sept 1811	cont'd
p76	#302	Whiteside	J.	pltfs bail		March 1812	cont'd
p76	#302	Richardson	Alex'r	defts bail		Sept 1812	cont'd
p76	#302	Lytle	Wm., Jr.	defts bail		Dec 1812	cont'd

MERO DISTRICT SUPERIOR COURT - 1810 - 1813

p76						May 1813	cont'd	Cause removed See #24
p76								
p76	#303	McAllister	Garland	plaintiff	detinue	March 1811	cont'd	
p76	#303	Nichols	John	defendant	non detinet	Sept 1811	cont'd	
p76	#303	Dixon	Tilman	pltfs bail	issue	March 1812	cont'd	
p76	#303	Scales	Joseph	defts bail		Sept 1812	cont'd	
p76						Dec 1812	cont'd	
p76						May 1813	jury/find for defendant/judgment for costs	
p76								
p76	#304	Hyde	Henry	plaintiff	debt	March 1811	cont'd	
p76	#304	Shute	Thomas	defendant	payment & issue	Sept 1811	jury/find for pltf/debt $200/damages $12.25	
p76	#304	Wharton	J.	pltfs bail				
p76	#304	Gordon	John	defts bail				
p77	#305	Hyde	Henry	plaintiff	debt	March 1811	plea payment & issue	
p77	#305	Shute	Thomas	defendant		Sept 1811	jury/ find for pltf/ debt $674.43/ damages $84.25	
p77	#305	Wharton	J	pltfs bail				
p77	#305	Gordon	John	defts bail				

MERO DISTRICT SUPERIOR COURT - 1810 - 1813

p77							
p77	#306	Hyde	Henry	plaintiff	debt	March 1811	cont'd
p77	#306	Hyde	Richard	pltf/admr	Demurrer/joinder	Sept 1811	cont'd
p77	#306	Erwin	Joseph	defendant		March 1812	cont'd
p77	#306	Wharton	J.	pltfs bail		Sept 1812	plaintiff' death suggested/cont'd
p77	#306	Craighead	John B.	defts bail		Dec 1812	suit continued in name of admr./demurrer overruled
p77							judgment for debt $200 with interest from 1 Sept 1800
p77	#307	Hyde	Henry	plaintiff	debt	March 1811	cont'd
p77	#307	Erwin	Joseph	defendant	Dem & joinder	Sept 1811	cont'd
p77	#307	Hyde	Richard	admr		March 1812	cont'd
p77	#307	Wharton	J.	pltfs bail		Sept 1812	pltfs death suggested/suit continued
p77	#307	Craighead	John B.	defts bail		Dec 1812	suit revived in name of admr/demurrer overruled/
p77							judgment for debt $874.43 & int from 8 Aug 1809 at 6%
p77							
p77	#308	Tayler	Joseph, Senr	plaintiff	case	March 1811	cont'd
p77	#308	Demoss	Lewis	defendant	not guilty/issue	Sept 1811	cont'd

MERO DISTRICT SUPERIOR COURT - 1810 - 1813

p77	#308	Demoss	Abraham	defendant		March 1812	cont'd
p77	#308	Demoss	John	defendant		Sept 1812	cont'd
p77	#308	Elliston	Hugh	pltfs bail		Dec 1812	cont'd
p77	#308	Tennisson	Sam'l	defts bail		May 1813	cont'd by consent cause removed See #25
p78	#309	Shepherd	Adam	plaintiff	case		
p78	#309	Sturgus	James A.	defendant	writ of enquiry	March 1811	judgment by default & writ of enquiry awarded
p78	#309	Drake	Robert	pltfs bail		Sept 1811	cont'd
p78	#309	Grundy	Felix	defts bail		March 1812	cont'd
p78	#309	Campbell	Mich'l	defts bail		Sept 1812	cont'd
p78	#309	Chasseze	Benj.	atty in fact		Dec 1812	dismissed/ B. Chasseze, atty in fact, for pltf/judg't for costs
p78							
p78	#310	Hartley	Charles	plaintiff	case	March 1811	Dem. & joinder/cont'd
p78	#310	Easten	Thomas	defendant	dem & joinder	Sept 1811	cont'd
p78	#310	Grundy	F.	pltfs bail		March 1812	
p78	#310	Easten	Wm	defts bail		Sept 1812	

112

MERO DISTRICT SUPERIOR COURT - 1810 - 1813

p78						Dec 1812	
p78						May 1813	demurrer overruled/writ of enquiry awarded/ cont'd
p78							cause removed See #26
p78							
p78	#311	Talbot	Clayton	plaintiff	case	March 1811	plea & issue
p78	#311	Dawns	James P.	defendant	not guilty/issue	Sept 1811	cont'd
p78	#311	Harvey	Thos.	pltfs bail		March 1812	cont'd
p78	#311	Criddle	John	defts bail		Sept 1812	cont'd
p78	#311	Tyree	Richardson	defts bail		Dec 1812	cont'd
p78						May 1813	cont'd by consent/ cause removed see #27
p78							
p78	#312	Thornton	Samuel	plaintiff	case	March 1811	plea
p78	#312	Downs	William	plaintiff	repn/issue	Sept 1811	cont'd
p78	#312	Overton	John	deft/admr		March 1812	cont'd
p78	#312	Mulherron	James	deft/admr		Sept 1812	cont'd
p78	#312	Ewing	Andrew	deft/admr		Dec 1812	cont'd

MERO DISTRICT SUPERIOR COURT - 1810 - 1813

p78	#312	Molloy	Thomas	deceased		May 1813	jury/Nonsuit/judgment for costs
p78	#312	Grundy	F.	pltfs bail			
p79	#313	Lytle	William, Jr.	plaintiff	debt	March 1811	issue
p79	#313	Hart	Robert W.	defendant	payment/issue	Sept 1811	jury/find for pltf/debt $400/damages $47
p79	#313	Dickenson	Jno.	pltfs bail			
p79							
p79	#314	Grimes	John A.	plaintiff	case	March 1811	Dem. & joinder
p79	#314	Easten	Thomas	defendant	dem. & joinder	Sept 1811	Shff released from not taking bail of deft/cont'd
p79	#314	Grundy	F.	pltfs bail		March 1812	cont'd
p79						Sept 1812	
p79						Dec 1812	Demurrer overruled/writ of Eng. awarded/cont'd
p79						May 1813	Demurrer withdrawn/cont'd
p79							Cause removed See #28
p79							
p79	#315	Warmack	Archer	plaintiff	debt		
p79	#315	Page	Absolom	defendant	payment/issue	March 1811	plea
p79	#315	Thomas	Jesse W.	defendant		Sept 1811	jury/find for pltf/debt $400/damages $41

MERO DISTRICT SUPERIOR COURT - 1810 - 1813

p79	#315	Grundy	F.	pltfs bail			
p79	#315	Barrow	Willie	defts bail			
p79	#315	Criddle	John	defts bail			
p79							
p79	#316	Goodwyn	Peterson	plaintiff	debt	March 1811	issue
p79	#316	Purnell	William	defendant	pay't/issue	Sept 1811	jury/find for pltf/debt $330.90/Damages $13.23
p79	#316	Wharton	J.	pltfs bail			judgment on costs/pltf returns $137.27
p79	#316	Saunders	Jolhn	defts bail			
p79	#316	Dismuke	Daniel	defts bail			
p80	#317	Waggoner	Michael	plaintiff	case	March 1811	order for alias capias
p80	#317	Kearney	Elijah	defendant		Sept 1811	cont'd
p80	#317	Young	Jno. L.	pltfs bail		March 1812	dismissed by pltf in proper person/deft assumes costs
p80	#317	Kearney	Vernon	defts bail			
p80							
p80	#318	Anderson	John	plaintiff	debt	March 1811	issue
p80	#318	Gordon	John	defendant	payment & issue	Sept 1811	jury/find for pltf/debt $2078.33/damages $148.19
p80	#318	Dickinson	John	pltfs bail			
p80	#318	Shute	Thos.	defts bail			
p80	#318	Tait	Wm	defts bail			
p80							

MERO DISTRICT SUPERIOR COURT   -   1810 - 1813

p80	#319	Anderson	John	plaintiff	debt	March 1811	issue
p80	#319	Gordon	John	defendant	payment & issue	Sept 1811	jury/find for p;ltf/debt $2078.33/damages $85.35
p80	#319	Dickinson	Jno	pltfs bail			
p80	#319	Shute	Thos.	defts bail			
p80	#319	Tait	Wm	defts bail			
p80							
p80	#320	Wilks	John	plaintiff	case	March 1811	cont'd
p80	#320	Nusam	Francis	defendant		Sept 1811	cont'd
p80	#320	Dupree	James	pltfs bail		March 1812	cont'd
p80	#320	Nusam	Eldridge	defts bail		Sept 1812	cont'd
p80						Dec 1812	cont'd
p80						May 1813	cont'd
p80							Cause removed See #29
p81	#321	Haywood	John	plaintiff	trespass	March 1811	judgment for deft & enquiry awarded
p81	#321	Grant	William	defendant	deflt/enquiry	Sept 1811	cont'd
p81	#321	Edmondson	Wm	pltfs bail		March 1812	cont'd

MERO DISTRICT SUPERIOR COURT - 1810 - 1813

p81	#321	Garrett	William	defts bail		Sept 1812	cont'd
p81						Dec 1812	cont'd
p81						May 1813	cont'd
p81							Cause removed See #30
p81							
p81	#322	Edwards	William	plaintiff	plea/non detinet	March 1811	venue changed on afft of pltf to Williamson
p81	#322	McConnell	John P.	defendant			
p81	#322	Tait	Wm	pltfs bail			
p81							
p81	#323	Anderson	John	plaintiff	debt	March 1811	issue
p81	#323	Josten	Benjamin	defendant	payment/issue	Sept 1811	jury/find for pltf/ debt $2078.33/damages $85.85
p81	#323	Dickinson	Jno	pltfs bail			
p81	#323	Rains	John	defts bail			
p81	#323	West	Geo.	defts bail			
p81							
p81	#324	Anderson	John	plaintiff	debt	March 1811	issue
p81	#324	Josten	Benjamin	defendant	payment/issue	Sept 1811	jury/find for pltf/debt $2078.33/damages $148.19
p81	#324	Dickinson	Jno	pltfs bail			
p81	#324	Rains	John	defts bail			
p81	#324	West	Geo.	defts bail			

MERO DISTRICT SUPERIOR COURT - 1810 - 1813

p82	#325	Anderson	John	plaintiff	debt	March 1811	issue
p82	#325	Joslin	Benjamin	defendant	payment/issue	Sept 1811	jury/ find for pltf/debt $753.34/damages $41.08
p82	#325	Dickinson	Jno	pltfs bail			
p82	#325	Rains	John	defts bail			
p82	#325	West	Geo.	defts bail			
p82							
p82	#326	Demoss	James	plaintiff	debt	March 1811	issue
p82	#326	Douglass	Ezekiel	defendant	payment/issue	Sept 1811	jury/ find for pltf/debt #775/damages $209.75
p82	#326	Dickinson	Jno.	pltfs bail			
p82							
p82	#327	Jackson	James	plaintiff	debt	March 1811	discontinued
p82	#327	Jackson	Washington	plaintiff			
p82	#327	Allen	Drury M.	defendant			
p82	#327	Dickinson	Jno	pltfs bail			
p82							
p82	#328	Potello	Catherine	plaintiff	covenant	March 1811	cont'd
p82	#328	Porter	Thomas	defendant	payment	Sept 1811	cont'd
p82	#328	Buck	John E.	pltfs bail		March 1812	cont'd
p82						Sept 1812	cont'd

MERO DISTRICT SUPERIOR COURT - 1810 - 1813

p82						Dec 1812	cont'd
p82						May 1813	cont'd
p82							Cause removed See #31
p83	#329	McBride	Samuel	plaintiff	case	March 1811	issue
p83	#329	Coleman	Joseph	defendant	non asst/issue	Sept 1811	cont'd
p83	#329	Dickinson	Jno	pltfs bail		March 1812	cont'd
p83						Sept 1812	cont'd
p83						Dec 1812	cont'd
p83						May 1813	jury/find for pltf/assess his damage to $342.12 & costs
p83							
p83	#330	Morrow	John	plaintiff	covenant	March 1811	dismissed//judgment for costs
p83	#330	Ewing	Ealey	defendant			
p83	#330	Grundy	Felix	pltfs bail			
p83							
p83	#331	Dillon	Thomas	plaintiff	case	March 1811	certiorari awarded
p83	#331	Bennet	Peter	defendant	non asst & issue	Sept 1811	cont'd

MERO DISTRICT SUPERIOR COURT - 1810 - 1813

p83						March 1812	cont'd by consent
p83						Sept 1812	cont'd
p83						Dec 1812	cont'd on afft of defendant
p83						May 1813	pltfs death suggested/cont't
p83							Cause removed See #32
p83							
p83	#332	Johnston	John	pltf/exor	covenant	March 1811	certerori awarded
p83	#332	Johnston	Alexander	deceased	cov't performed	Sept 1811	defendant being dead/suit continued in name of exor.
p83	#332	Dew	Arthur	deft/admr		March 1812	cont'd
p83	#332	Dew	Susannah	deft/wife		Sept 1812	cont'd
p83	#332	Harris	Tyree	deceased		Dec 1812	cont'd
p83						May 1813	cont'd on defts afft
p83							Cause removed See #33
p84	#333	Dupree	Nancy	plaintiff	petition for divorce	March 1811	order to issue
p84	#333	Nichols	John	next friend		Sept 1811	dismissed by the pltfs next friend
p84	#333	Dupree	James	defendant			

120

MERO DISTRICT SUPERIOR COURT - 1810 - 1813

p84							
p84	#334	Blount	Willie [Gov.]	plaintiff	debt	March 1811	judgment on motion of Thos. Crutcher, Treasurer, for
p84	#334	Cheatham	John B. [shff & Col.]	defendant	Robertson Co.		$465.67 the balance of the State Tax for 1809 & costs
p84	#334	Brooks	John	security			
p84	#334	Windfield	Joseph	security			
p84	#334	Tolar	Robert	security			
p84	#334	Casselberry	Joseph	security			
p84							
p84	#335	Blount	Willie [Gov.]	plaintiff	debt	March 1811	judgment on motion of Thos. Crutcher, Treasurer, for
p84	#335	King	William [shff & Col.]	defendant	Franklin Co.		$192. the State Tax for 1808 & costs
p84	#335	Bullard	Joseph	security			
p84	#335	Wiggen	Thos. D.	security			
p84							
p84	#336	Blount	Willie [Gov.]	plaintiff	debt	March 1811	judgment on motion of Thos. Crutcher, Treasurer, for
p84	#336	King	William [shff & Col.]	defendant	Franklin Co.		$233.72 the State Tax for year 1809 & costs
p84	#336	Russell	James	security			
p84	#336	Bullard	Joseph	security			
p85	#337	Blount	Willie [Gov.]	plaintiff	debt	March 1811	judgment on motion of Thos Crutcher, Treasurer,
p85	#337	Phillips	William [shff & col.	defendant	White Co.		for $231.47 the State Tax for the year 1809 & costs

MERO DISTRICT SUPERIOR COURT   -   1810 - 1813

p85	#337	White	John	security			
p85	#337	McDaniel	David	security			
p85	#337	Lane	Jacob A.	security			
p85							
p85	#338	Blount	Willie [Gov.]	plaintiff	debt		March 1811 judgment on motion of Thos. Crutcher, Treasurer, for
p85	#338	Phillips	William [shff & col.] defendant		White Co.		$180.55 the balance of the State Tax for the year 1810
p85	#338	Laurey	Alexander	security			
p85	#338	Lane	Jacob A.	security			
p85	#338	Carrick	John M.	security			
p85	#338	Gist	William	security			
p85							
p85	#339	Blount	Willie [Gov.]	plaintiff	debt		March 1811 judgment on motion of Thos. Cruther, Treasurer, for
p85	#339	Griffin	John [shff & Col]	defendant	Rutherford Co.		$592.27 the balance of the State Tax for the year 1809
p85	#339	Pitteway	Hincky	security			
p85	#339	Dyer	Robert H.	security			
p85	#339	Jenkins	Nimrod	security			
p85	#339	Mitchell	William	security			
p85	#339	Bean	Jesse	security			
p85							
p85	#340	Blount	Willie [Gov]	plaintiff	debt		March 1811 judgment on motion of Thos. Crutcher, Treasurer, for
p85	#340	Griffin	John [shff & Col]	defendant	Rutherford Co.		$706.83, the State Tax for the year 1810 & costs
p85	#340	Mitchell	William	security			

MERO DISTRICT SUPERIOR COURT - 1810 - 1813

p85	#340	Dyer	Robert H.	security			
p85	#340	McCulloch	Alexander	security			
p85	#340	LeGrand	Peter	security			
p86	#341	Hamilton	James	plaintiff	Scifa	Sept 1811	judgment according to scifa
p86	#341	Clark	David	defendant			
p86	#341	Gordon	John	defts bond			
p86							
p86	#342	Blair	John	plaintiff	certerari	Sept 1811	cont'd
p86	#342	Richardson	Elijah	defendant		March 1812	cont'd
p86						Sept 1812	cont'd
p86						Dec 1812	cont'd
p86						May 1813	jury/special verdict/cont'd
p86							Cause removed See #34
p86							
p86	#343	Pipkins	Philip	plaintiff	covenant	Sept 1811	cont'd
p86	#343	Stewart	Peter B.	defendant	certeorari	March 1812	cont'd
p86					cov't performed	Sept 1812	cont'd
p86						Dec 1812	cont'd

MERO DISTRICT SUPERIOR COURT - 1810 - 1813

p86						May 1813	jury/find for pltf/$205.35 & costs
p86							judgment of the county court affirmed
p86							
p86	#344	Wade	William H.	plaintiff	case	Sept 1811	dismissed/judgment
p86	#344	Wade	Judith L.	plaintiff			
p86	#344	Douglass	James	next friend			
p86	#344	Prout	Joshua	defendant			
p87	#345	Anderson	John	plaintiff	Scifa	Sept 1811	cont'd
p87	#345	Mahan	Wm A.	defendant	payment/issue	March 1812	cont'd
p87	#345	Williamson	John S.	defts bail		Sept 1812	cont'd
p87	#345	Laird	Alexander	defts bail		Dec 1812	cont'd
p87						May 1813	jury/say deft has not paid the debt in the Scifa
p87							judgment of the county court affirmed
p87							
p87	#346	Jackson	James	plaintiff	Scifa appl	Sept 1811	cont'd
p87	#346	Jackson	Washington	plaintiff	payment/issue	March 1812	cont'd
p87	#346	Griggs	Real	defendant		Sept 1812	cont'd

MERO DISTRICT SUPERIOR COURT - 1810 - 1813

p87	#346	Beck	John E.	pltfs bail		Dec 1812	cont'd
p87						May 1813	dismissed/deft assumes the costs
p87							
p87	#347	Harman	Richard	plaintiff	debt	Sept 1811	jury/find for pltf $398.52 debt/damages $32.54
p87	#347	Jackson	Henry	defendant	pay't/issue		
p87							
p87	#348	Cheatham	Archer	plaintiff	Scifa appl	Sept 1811	cont'd
p87	#348	Kile	William	defendant	pay't/issue	March 1812	
p87	#348	Whiteside	Jenkin	security		Sept 1812	
p87	#348	Searcy	Robert	security		Dec 1812	
p87						May 1813	
p87							Cause removed See #35
p88	#349	Chandler	Isaac	plaintiff	case appl	Sept 1811	motion by deft to change the venue/cont'd on the petition & afft of deft/ trial be adjourned to the next Circuit Court of the county of Rutherford
p88	#349	Kibble	Walter	defendant	non-culpabilities	March 1812	
p88					issue		
p88							
p88	#350	Roper/Rosser	William	plaintiff	appl	Sept 1811	cont'd

125

MERO DISTRICT SUPERIOR COURT - 1810 - 1813

p88	#350	McDaniel	Clement	defendant		March 1812	cont'd
p88						Sept 1812	cont'd
p88						Dec 1812	cont'd
p88						May 1813	jury/ find for pltf/ $23.86
p88							
p88	#351	Porter	Alexander, Senr	plaintiff	Scifa appl	Sept 1811	cont'd
p88	#351	Porter	Alexander, Junr	plaintiff	payment	March 1812	cont'd
p88	#351	Mahan	Wm A.	defendant	surrender	Sept 1812	cont'd
p88	#351	Bradford	Benjamin J.	defts bail	rep'n & issues	Dec 1812	cont'd
p88						May 1813	jury/find the deft has not paid the debt on Scifa or surrendered sd Mahan/
p88							judgment of county court affirmed
p88							
p88	#352	Bevins	Fielder	plaintiff	Scifa	Sept 1811	judg on repl. bond
p88	#352	Kelton	Wm	defendant		March 1812	cont'd
p88	#352	Wilson	James			Sept 1812	cont'd
p88						Dec 1812	cont'd

MERO DISTRICT SUPERIOR COURT - 1810 - 1813

p88						May 1813	Scifa dismissed/ deft to pay costs
p89	#353	Moore	Edward	plaintiff	Scifa	Sept 1811	judgment on repl bond
p89	#353	Kelton	Wm	defendant		March 1812	cont'd
p89	#353	Wilson	James	defendant		Sept 1812	cont'd
p89						Dec 1812	cont'd
p89						May 1813	dismissed/judgment agst deft for costs
p89							
p89	#354	Hobbs	Joel	plaintiff	debt	Sept 1811	jury/ find for pltf/ $60 debt/ Damages $2
p89	#354	Erwin	John	defendant			judgment of the county court affirmed
p89	#354	Robertson	Sterling C.	defendant			
p89							
p89	#355	Stump	John	plaintiff	case appl	Sept 1811	venue canged to Williamson Co. Circuit Ct by pltf
p89	#355	Young	John L.	defendant	not guilty/issue justification		deft files a bill of exceptions
p89							
p89							
p89	#356	Stump	John	plaintiff	case appl	Sept 1811	venue changed to Williamson Circuit Ct by pltf
p89	#356	Young	Daniel	defendant	not guilty/issue repns & issue		deft files bill of exceptions
p89							

MERO DISTRICT SUPERIOR COURT - 1810 - 1813

p90	#357	Claiborne	Ferdinand L.	plaintiff	debt		Sept 1811	judg by default & debt $322.12 & int. from 10 Nov 1808
p90	#357	Ross	Daniel	defendant				
p90	#357	Grundy	F.	pltfs bail				
p90	#357	Napier	Rich'd C.	defts bail				
p90	#357	Goldsberry	J. B.	defts bail				
p90								
p90	#358	Tyrrell	James	plaintiff	case		Sept 1811	issue alias
p90	#358	Kerr	Joseph	defendant			March 1812	cont'd
p90							Sept 1812	cont'd
p90							Dec 1812	cont'd
p90							May 1813	dismissed/judgment for costs
p90								
p90	#359	McCance	Matthew	plaintiff	trespass		Sept 1811	plea not guilty & issue
p90	#359	Adams	Robert	defendant	not guilty/issue		March 1812	cont'd
p90	#359	Douglass	Hugh	pltfs bail			Sept 1812	cont'd
p90	#359	Terrill	James	defts bail			Dec 1812	cont'd
p90	#359	Childress	N. G.	defts bail			May 1813	Nonsuit/judgment for costs/rule to set aside Nonsuit
p90								Nonsuit set aside/new trial granted/cont'd

MERO DISTRICT SUPERIOR COURT - 1810 - 1813

p90							Cause removed See #36
p90							
p90	#360	White	John	plaintiff	covenant	Sept 1811	oyer/plead so as not to delay trial
p90	#360	Anderson	William P.	defendant	repn/issue	March 1812	pleas issue/cont'd
p90	#360	Grundy	F.	pltfs bail	demurrer/joinder	Sept 1812	cont'd
p90	#360	Hall	E. S.	defts bail		Dec 1812	cont'd
p90						May 1813	cont'd
p90							Cause removed See #37
p91	#361	Poole	Marthy Jefferson Petty	plaintiff	detinue	Sept 1811	plea
p91	#361	PettyPoole	Marthy Jefferson	plaintiff	non detinue	March 1812	cont'd
p91	#361	Malone	Booth	next friend	issue	Sept 1812	costs of suit paid & to be dismissed next term
p91	#361	Jackson	James	defendant		Dec 1812	dismissed/judgment for costs
p91	#361	Figures	Matthew	pltfs bail			
p91	#361	Maderson	Thos.	defts bail			
p91	#361	Deaderick	Thos.				
p91							
p91	#362	Whiteside	Jenkin	plaintiff	decta	Sept 1811	plea

MERO DISTRICT SUPERIOR COURT - 1810 - 1813

p91	#362	Cobb	Joseph	defendant	not guilty/issue	March 1812	cont'd
p91	#362	Hayes	O. B.	pltfs bail		Sept 1812	cont'd
p91	#362	Greer	Joseph	defts bail		Dec 1812	cont'd
p91	#362	Teel	Edw'd	defts bail		May 1813	cont'd by consent
p91							cause removed See #38
p91							
p91	#363	Winchester & Cage		plaintiff	debt	Sept 1811	judgment confessed by deft for debt $170.07/$40 damages
p91	#363	Seawell	Benjamin	defendant			
p91	#363	Wharton	J.	pltfs bail			
p91	#363	Seawell	Thos.	defts bail			
p91	#363	Morgan	Wm C.	defts bail			
p91							
p91	#364	Niel	Thomas H.	plaintiff	debt	Sept 1811	judgment by default/writ of enquiry awarded
p91	#364	Robertson	Thompson	defendant			
p91	#364	Turnstall	Edward	defendant			
p91	#364	Grundy	F.	pltfs bail	writ of enquiry	March 1812	cont'd
p91	#364	Bradford	Benjamin J.	defts bail		Sept 1812	
p91	#364	Roper	Wm	defts bail		Dec 1812	jury/assess pltfs damages to $82.92

MERO DISTRICT SUPERIOR COURT   -   1810 - 1813

p92	#365	Newnam	John	plaintiff	Demurrer	Sept 1811	leave granted pltf to amend the writ/cont'd
p92	#365	McNairy	Boyd	defendant		March 1812	cont'd
p92	#365	Ringue	James B.	pltfs bail		Sept 1812	cont'd
p92	#365	Beck	John E.	defts bail		Dec 1812	cont'd
p92	#365	McNairy	N. A.	defts bail		May 1813	demurrer withdrawn/cont'd
p92							cause removed See #39
p92							
p92	#366	Barry	Redmond D.	plaintiff	case	Sept 1811	cont'd
p92	#366	Trigg	William, Junr	defendant		March 1812	cont'd
p92	#366	Dergin	John	pltfs bail		Sept 1812	cont'd
p92	#366	Weakley	Robert	defts bail		Dec 1812	cont'd
p92	#366	Payton	John	defts bail		May 1813	cont'd
p92							cause removed See #40
p92							
p92	#367	Williamson	John S.	plaintiff	case	Sept 1811	issue alias on Jno Mitchell
p92	#367	Neilson	Charles B.	defendant		March 1812	cont'd

MERO DISTRICT SUPERIOR COURT - 1810 - 1813

p92	#367	Mitchell	John	defendant	[not found]	Sept 1812	cont'd
p92	#367	Williamson	Thos.	pltfs bail		Dec 1812	cont'd
p92	#367	Stothart	Robt	defts bail		May 1813	cont'd
p92							cause removed See #41
p92							
p92	#368	Blount	Willie [Gov]	plaintiff	debt	Sept 1811	judgt on motion for $307.30/balance of state tax of 1810
p92	#368	Statler	Cornelius [sheriff]	defendant			for Lincoln County
p92							
p92	#369	Blount	Willie [Gov]	plaintiff	debt	Sept 1811	judgt on motion for $90.68/balance to state tax for 1810 for Bedford County
p92	#369	Moore	Thos. [county court clerk]				
p93	#370	Burnett & Raymond		plaintiff	Scifa	Sept 1811	issue
p93	#370	Stephens	Robert	defendant		March 1812	cont'd
p93						Sept 1812	Dismissed/deft assumes the cost
p93							
p93	#371	Ingram	Francis	plaintiff	certerari	March 1812	motion to dismiss the certerari/cont'd
p93	#371	Cabaness	Charles	defendant	petition to share	Sept 1812	cont'd
p93					estate	Dec 1812	cont'd

MERO DISTRICT SUPERIOR COURT - 1810 - 1813

p93						May 1813	motion to dismiss/cont'd
p93							Cause removed See #42
p93							
p93	#372	Howser	Jacob	plaintiff	certerari	March 1812	cont'd
p93	#372	Glass	John	defendant		Sept 1812	cont'd
p93	#372	Hays	Andrew	defendant		Dec 1812	cont'd
p93						May 1813	jury/ find for the pltf/ $48.20
p93							
p93	#373	Thomas	Phinehas	pltf/exor	debt	March 1812	cont'd
p93	#373	Scruggs	Finch	pltf/exor	certiorari	Sept 1812	cont'd
p93	#373	Thomas	Jesse	deceased	paym't set off	Dec 1812	cont'd
p93	#373	Thomas	Jesse W.	defendant	issues	May 1813	cont'd on aff't of defts atty
p93							cause removed See #43
p94	#374	Childress	John	pltf/exor	debt appl	March 1812	cont'd
p94	#374	Childress	Thomas	pltf/exor	pay't set off &	Sept 1812	cont'd
p94	#374	Hickman	Thos.	pltf/exor	issues	Dec 1812	jury/find for pltf/debt $144.9/damages $15.44

MERO DISTRICT SUPERIOR COURT   -   1810 - 1813

p94	#374	Childress	John	deceased			judgment of the county court affirmed
p94	#374	Sappington	Roger B.	defendant			
p94							
p94	#375	Horton	Josiah	plaintiff	debt appl	March 1812	deft withdraws his pleas & confesses judg't for the amount of the County Court/
p94	#375	McNairy	Nathaniel A.	defendant	payment set off		judgment accordingly
p94					repn & issues		
p94							
p94	#376	Brown	William	plaintiff	debt appl	March 1812	cont'd
p94	#376	Parker	Isham A.	defendant	payment set off	Sept 1812	the debt & costs being paid pltf intends no further
p94					repn & issues		to prosecute
p94							
p94	#377	Roper	William	plaintiff	In error	March 1812	cont'd
p94	#377	Stone	William	defendant		Sept 1812	cont'd
p94						Dec 1812	cont'd
p94						May 1813	cont'd
p94							Cause removed See #44
p95	#378	Pullain	Drury	plaintiff	debt appl	March 1812	cont'd
p95	#378	Robertson	William B.	defendant	paym't set off	Sept 1812	cont'd

MERO DISTRICT SUPERIOR COURT - 1810 - 1813

p95					repn & issues	Dec 1812	jury/find for pltf/debt $832.76/damages $31.80
p95							judgement of the county court affirmed
	#379	Cantrell	Stephen, Jr.	plaintiff	an appeal	March 1812	cont'd
	#379	Pryor	Susannah	deft/admx		Sept 1812	cont'd
p95		Pryor	Sam'l	deceased		Dec 1812	cont'd
p95						May 1813	jury/Nonsuit/rule to set Nonsuit aside/Nonsuit set aside
p95							cont'd/pltf ordered to pay cost of this term
p95							Cause removed See #45
p95							
p95	#380	Helm	John	plaintiff	debt	March 1812	cont'd
p95	#380	Campbell	Michael	defendant	ready to perform	Sept 1812	cont'd
p95						Dec 1812	cont'd
p95						May 1813	demurrer sustained & issues cont'd
p95							Cause removed See #46
p95							
p95	#381	Hickman	Thomas	plaintiff	an appeal	March 1812	defendants death suggested/cont'd
p95	#381	Brooks	Matthew	defendant		Sept 1812	ordered suit be revived in name of administrators/cont'd

MERO DISTRICT SUPERIOR COURT - 1810 - 1813

p95	#381	Brooks	Robert	deft/admr		Dec 1812	cont'd
p95	#381	Brooks	Arthur	deft/admr		May 1813	cont'd on affdt of one of the defts
p95	#381	Brooks	John	deft/admr			Cause removed See #47
p96	#382	Stump	John	plaintiff	an appl	March 1812	cont'd
p96	#382	Brooks	Matthew	defendant		Sept 1812	defendant being dead/suit continued in name of admrs.
p96	#382	Brooks	Robert	deft/admr		Dec 1812	cont'd
p96	#382	Brooks	Arthur	deft/admr		May 1812	jury/find for pltf/$15.41/judgment of county court affrmd
p96	#382	Brooks	John	deft/admr			
p96							
p96	#383	Marr	George W. L.	plaintiff	debt appl	March 1812	cont'd
p96	#383	Bradford	Thomas G.	defendant	payment set off	Sept 1812	cont'd
p96					repn & issues	Dec 1812	jury/find for pltf/debt $304.83/damages $10.78
p96							judgment of the county court affirmed
p96							
p96	#384	Jackson	James	plaintiff	debt appl	March 1812	cont'd
p96	#384	Jackson	Washington	plaintiff	payment/issues	Sept 1812	

MERO DISTRICT SUPERIOR COURT - 1810 - 1813

p96	#384	Bell	Hugh F.	defendant		Dec 1812	jury/find for pltf/debt $516.57/damages $16.34
p96							judgment of the county court affirmed
p96							
p96	#385	Brown	William	plaintiff	debt appl	March 1812	cont'd
p96	#385	Bell	Hugh F.	defendant	payment/issue	Sept 1812	
p96						Dec 1812	jury/find for pltf/debt $215.67/damages $14.96
p96							judgment of the county court affirmed
p97	#386	Tiernan	Luke	plaintiff	debt appl	March 1812	cont'd
p97	#386	Bell	Hugh F.	defendant	payn't/issue	Sept 1812	cont'd
p97		Dickenson	Jno.	Atty		Dec 1812	cont'd
p97						May 1813	plea withdrawn/judg't agst principal & securities/12% int.
p97							
p97	#387	Tiernan	Luke	plaintiff	debt appl	March 1812	cont'd
p97	#387	Bell	Hugh F.		paym't/issue	Sept 1812	cont'd
p97	#387	Dickinson	Jno	Atty		Dec 1812	cont'd
p97						May 1813	plea withdrawn/judg't agst principal & securities/12%int.

MERO DISTRICT SUPERIOR COURT - 1810 - 1813

p97								
p97	#388	Litton	Susannah	pltf/admx	in error		March 1812	cont'd
p97	#388	Litton	Jasper	pltf/admr	errors assigned		Sept 1812	cont'd
p97	#388	Pryor	Sam'l	deceased			Dec 1812	cont'd
p97	#388	Kenisse	Edward	defendant			May 1813	by consent this suit is adjourned to the next Supreme
p97								Court of Errors & Appeals for the 4th Circuit
p97								
p97	#389	Harding	Edward	plaintiff	case appl		March 1812	cont'd
p97	#389	Cox	John L.	deft/admr	non asst/set off		Sept 1812	cont'd
p97	#389	Phillips	Eliza	deft/admx	issues		Dec 1812	cont'd
p97	#389	Phillips	Merrel	deceased			May 1813	dismissed by plty/judgment for costs
p98	#390	Schroeder	Henry	plaintiff	debt appl		March 1812	cont'd
p98	#390	Perkins	William	defendant	pay't set off		Sept 1812	cont'd
p98					repn & issues		Dec 1812	cont'd
p98							May 1813	plea withdrawn/judgment principal & securities 12% int.

138

MERO DISTRICT SUPERIOR COURT - 1810 - 1813

p98							
p98	#391	Watkins	Isaac	plaintiff	debt appl	March 1812	on defts petition & affdvt case adjourned to the next Circuit Court for the County of Wilson
p98	#391	Boyd	Richard	defendant	plea		
p98					repn & issues		
p98							
p98	#392	Schroeder	Henry	plaintiff	debt appl	March 1812	cont'd
p98	#392	Robertson	Wm		paym't/ set off	Sept 1812	cont'd
p98					repn & issues	Dec 1812	cont'd
p98						May 1813	plea withdrawn/payment agst principal & securities at 12%
p98							
p98	#393	Poyzer	George	plaintiff	debt appl	March 1812	cont'd
p98	#393	Purnell	William	defendant	decta demurrer	Sept 1812	cont'd
p98					& joinder	Dec 1812	cont'd
p98						May 1813	demurrer overruled/judgment of the county court affirmed
p99	#394	Poyzer	George	plaintiff	debt appl	March 1812	cont'd
p99	#394	Purnell	William	defendant	decta demurrer	Sept 1812	cont'd

MERO DISTRICT SUPERIOR COURT - 1810 - 1813

p99					& joinder	Dec 1812	cont'd
p99						May 1813	demurrer overruled/judg't of county court affirmed
p99							
p99	#395	Lytle	William, Junr	plaintiff	debt appl	March 1812	cont'd
p99	#395	Perkins	Thomas H.	defendant	payment/set off	Sept 1812	cont'd
p99					& issue	Dec 1812	cont'd
p99						May 1813	jury/finds for pltf/ $1033.77/judgment affirmed
p99							
p99	#396	Smith	John H.	plaintiff	case appl	March 1812	cont'd
p99	#396	Lewis	William T.	defendant	non asst/issue	Sept 1812	cont'd
p99						Dec 1812	cont'd
p99						May 1813	defts death suggested/Scifa to issue agst his executors
p99							cause removed See #48
p99							
p99	#397	Crow	Joshua	plaintiff	debt	March 1812	judgment by default/$299.13 with interest
p99	#397	Stump	John	defendant			
p99	#397	Grundy	Felix	pltfs bail			

MERO DISTRICT SUPERIOR COURT - 1810 - 1813

p100	#398	Childress	Nathaniel G.	plaintiff	AB	March 1812	cont'd
p100	#398	Goodrich	Edmund	defendant		Sept 1812	cont'd
p100	#398	Goodrich	John	defts bail		Dec 1812	cont'd
p100	#398	Barrow	Willie	defts bail		May 1813	cont'd
p100	#398	Taylor	Sam'l	pltfs bail			cause removed See #49
p100							
p100	#399	Hughes	William	plaintiff	cases	March 1812	cont'd
p100	#399	Stump	Frederick	defendant	non asst/issues	Sept 1812	cont'd
p100	#399	Haywood	J.	pltfs bail		Dec 1812	leave granted pltf to amend his dicta./cont'd
p100						May 1813	ordered pltf pay all the cost of his own witnesses/cont'd
p100							cause removed See #50
p100							
p100	#400	Jackson	Samuel	plaintiff	cases	March 1812	cont'd
p100	#400	Watkins	Thomas G.	defendant		Sept 1812	cont'd
p100	#400	Jackson	Henry	pltfs bail		Dec 1812	cont'd
p100	#400	Dickinson	John	defts bail		May 1813	cont'd
p100	#400	McNairy	Boyd	defts bail			cause removed See #51

MERO DISTRICT SUPERIOR COURT   -   1810 - 1813

p100							
p100	#401	Turner	William	plaintiff	AB	March 1812	dismissed by the pltfs atty and deft assumes the costs
p100	#401	Carroll	William	defendant			
p100	#401	Pilcher	Joshua	pltfs bail			
p100	#401	Hynes	And'w	defts bail			
p100	#401	Shackleford	Thos	defts bail			
p101	#402	Robertson	William B.	plaintiff	plea in abatement	March 1812	cont'd
p101	#402	Wilson	Nicholas	defendant		Sept 1812	cont'd
p101	#402	Buck	John E.	pltfs bail		Dec 1812	cont'd
p101	#402	Dickinson	Jno	defts bail		May 1813	cause removed See #52
p101	#402	Hamilton	Jno B.	defts bail			
p101							
p101	#403	Den	John	lessee	eject.	March 1812	cont'd
p101	#403	McGavock	James	owner	plea/not guilty	Sept 1812	cont'd
p101	#403	Hinton	Jeremiah	defendant	& issues	Dec 1812	cont'd
p101						May 1813	cont'd by consent/ Cause removed See #53
p101							
p101	#404	Den	John	lessee	eject.	March 1812	cont'd

142

MERO DISTRICT SUPERIOR COURT   -   1810 - 1813

p101	#404	McGavock	James	owner	plea/not guilty	Sept 1812	cont'd
p101	#404	Talbot	Thomas	defendant	& issue	Dec 1812	cont'd
p101						May 1813	cont'd by consent // See #54
p101							
p101	#405	Rowlandson	Sam'l	plaintiff	case	March 1812	cont'd
p101	#405	Brien	Edw'd	plaintiff		Sept 1812	cont'd
p101	#405	Brien	Isaac	plaintiff		Dec 1812	cont'd
p101	#405	Brien	William	plaintiff		May 1813	cont'd // Cause removed See #55
p101	#405	Burland	Thomas [alias]	defendant			
p101	#405	McBurland	Thomas	defendant			
p101	#405	Anderson	Wm P.	pltfs bail			
p102	#406	Penfold	John	plaintiff	case	March 1812	cont'd
p102	#406	Somer	Joseph	plaintiff		Sept 1812	cont'd
p102	#406	Burland	Thomas [alias]	defendant		Dec 1812	cont'd
p102	#406	Burland	Thomas M.	defendant		May 1813	cont'd // Cause removed See #56
p102	#406	Anderson	William P.	pltfs bail			
p102							

MERO DISTRICT SUPERIOR COURT - 1810 - 1813

p102	#407	Langster	Alexander	plaintiff	case	March 1812	cont'd
p102	#407	Atkinson	George	plaintiff		Sept 1812	cont'd
p102	#407	Taylor	David	plaintiff		Dec 1812	cont'd
p102	#407	Burland	Thomas [alias]	defendant		May 1813	cont'd Cause Removed See #57
p102	#407	Burland	Thomas M.	defendant			
p102	#407	Anderson	William P.	pltfs bail			
p102							
p102	#408	Pritchard	Richard P.	plaintiff	case	March 1812	cont'd
p102	#408	Pearson	John	plaintiff		Sept 1812	cont'd
p102	#408	Alderson	Christopher	plaintiff		Dec 1812	cont'd
p102	#408	Burland	Thomas [alias]	defendant		May 1813	cont'd // Cause removed See #58
p102	#408	Burland	Thomas M.	defendant			
p102	#408	Anderson	William P.	pltfs bail			
p102							
p102	#409	Turner	John	plaintiff	case	March 1812	cont'd
p102	#409	Whiteside	Geo.	plaintiff		Sept 1812	cont'd
p102	#409	Turner	Skinner	plaintiff		Dec 1812	cont'd

MERO DISTRICT SUPERIOR COURT - 1810 - 1813

p102	#409	Burland	Thomas als	defendant		May 1813	cont'd // See #59
p102	#409	Burland	Thomas M.	defendant			
p102	#409	Anderson	William P.	pltfs bail			
p103	#410	Turner	Skinner	plaintiff	case	March 1812	cont'd
p103	#410	Docker	Edmund	plaintiff		Sept 1812	cont'd
p103	#410	Draper	Daniel	plaintiff		Dec 1812	cont'd
p103	#410	Anderson	Wm P.	pltfs bail		May 1813	cont'd // Cause removed/ see #60
p103	#410	Burland	Thomas alias	defendant			
p103	#410	Burland	Thomas M.	defendant			
p103							
p103	#411	Williams	Thomas	plaintiff	case	March 1812	cont'd
p103	#411	Burland	Thomas alias	defendant		Sept 1812	cont'd
p103	#411	Burland	Thomas M.	defendant		Dec 1812	cont'd
p103	#411	Anderson	William P.	pltfs bail		May 1813	cont'd // Cause removed See #61
p103							
p103	#412	Duckham	Joseph	plaintiff	case	March 1812	cont'd
p103	#412	Lankester	Robert	plaintiff		Sept 1812	cont'd

MERO DISTRICT SUPERIOR COURT - 1810 - 1813

p103	#412	Burland	Thomas alias	defendant		Dec 1812	cont'd
p103	#412	Burland	Thomas M.	defendant		May 1813	cont'd // Cause removed See #62
	#412	Anderson	William P.	pltfs bail			
p103							
p103	#413	Smith	William	plaintiff	case	March 1812	cont'd
p103	#413	Henderson	James	plaintiff		Sept 1812	cont'd
p103	#413	Burland	Thomas alias	defendant		Dec 1812	cont'd
p103	#413	Burland	Thomas M.	defendant		May 1813	cont'd // Cause removed / See #63
p103	#413	Anderson	William P.	pltfs bail			
p104	#414	Neale	John	plaintiff	case	March 1812	cont'd
p104	#414	Perkins	Wright	plaintiff		Sept 1812	cont'd
p104	#414	Perkins	Joseph	plaintiff		Dec 1812	cont'd
p104	#414	Burland	Thomas alias	defendant		May 1813	cont'd // Cause removed See #64
p104	#414	Burland	Thomas M.	defendant			
p104	#414	Anderson	Wm P.	pltfs bail			
p104							
p104	#415	Parks	Thomas	plaintiff	case	March 1812	cont'd

MERO DISTRICT SUPERIOR COURT - 1810 - 1813

p104	#415	Burland	Thomas alias	defendant		Sept 1812	cont'd
p104	#415	Burland	Thomas M.	defendant		Dec 1812	cont'd
p104	#415	Anderson	Wm P.	pltfs bail		May 1813	cont'd // Cause removed See #65
p104							
p104	#416	Cooper	John	plaintiff	case	March 1812	cont'd
p104	#416	Burland	Thomas alias	defendant		Sept 1812	cont'd
p104	#416	Burland	Thomas M.	defendant		Dec 1812	cont'd
p104	#416	Anderson	Wm P.	pltfs bail		May 1813	cont'd // Cause removed See #66
p104							
p104	#417	Gordon	John	plaintiff	case	March 1812	judg't confessed for $4663.19 & costs/judg't accordingly
p104	#417	Pickering	John T.	defendant			[executed & deft committed to jail]
p105	#418	Wilson	John, Senr	plaintiff	case	March 1812	cont'd //Cause removed / See #67
p105	#418	Wilson	John, Junr	plaintiff		Sept 1812	cont'd
p105	#418	Wilson	Nicholas	plaintiff		Dec 1812	cont'd
p105	#418	Burland	Thomas alias	defendant		May 1813	cont'd
p105	#418	Burland	Thomas M.	defendant			

MERO DISTRICT SUPERIOR COURT   -   1810 - 1813

p105	#418	Anderson	Wm P.	pltfs bail				
p105								
p105	#419	Williamson	John L.	plaintiff	petition	March 1812	motion to dismiss by pltfs atty/cont'd	
p105	#419	Sommerville	John	defendant		Sept 1812	cont'd	
p105	#419	Searcy	Bennet	defendant		Dec 1812	cont'd	
p105	#419	Searcy	Robert	defendant		May 1813	cont'd //Cause removed / See #68	
p105								
p105	#420	Bell	Henry	plaintiff	petition	March 1812	cont'd	
p105	#420	Sommerville	John	defendant		Sept 1812	cont'd	
p105	#420	Searcy	Bennet	defendant		Dec 1812	cont'd	
p105	#420	Searcy	Robert	defendant		May 1813	cont'd // Cause removed / See #69	
p105								
p105	#421	Purvis	Allen	plaintiff	petition	March 1812	cont'd	
p105	#421	Gordon	John	defendant		Sept 1812	cont'd	
p105	#421	Tait	William	defendant		Dec 1812	cont'd	
p105	#421	Searcy	Bennet	defendant		May 1813	cont'd // Cause removed / See #70	

MERO DISTRICT SUPERIOR COURT - 1810 - 1813

p106	#422	Elliston	Joseph T.	pltf/admr	petition	March 1812	cont'd
p106	#422	Mullen	Mary	pltf/admx		Sept 1812	cont'd
p106	#422	Mullen	William	deceased		Dec 1812	cont'd
p106	#422	Gordon	John	defendant		May 1813	cont'd // Cause removed / See #71
p106	#422	Tait	William	defendant			
p106	#422	Perkins	Thos. H.	defendant			
p106							
p106	#423	Lyle	George	plaintiff	petition	March 1812	cont'd // Cause removed / See #72
p106	#423	Gordon	John	defendant		Sept 1812	cont'd
p106	#423	Perkins	Thos. H.	defendant		Dec 1812	cont'd
p106	#423	Searcy	Bennet	defendant		May 1813	cont'd
p106							
p106	#424	Childress	Henry	plaintiff	covenant appl	Sept 1812	cont'd
p106	#424	May	Francis	defendant		Dec 1812	cont'd
p106						May 1813	cont'd // Cause removed - See #73
p106							
p106	#425	Brady [case X'd out]	William	plaintiff	debt	Sept 1812	cont'd

MERO DISTRICT SUPERIOR COURT - 1810 - 1813

p106	#425	Henderson	William T.	defendant		Dec 1812	cont'd
p106						May 1813	plea withdrawn/judg't agst deft & surity for int. only
p106							by consent
p107	#426	Williams [case X'd out]	Robert C.	plaintiff	petition	March 1812	
p107	#426	McGavock	David [register of W TN]	defendant			
p107							
p107	#427	Miller	Jane	plaintiff	divorce petition	Sept 1812	Alias subpoena to issue / cont'd
p107	#427	Porter	Thomas	next friend		Dec 1812	order for publication in *Clarian* // cont'd
p107	#427	Miller	Jacob	defendant		May 1813	Decree she be divorced & that she pay costs for petition
p107							
p107	#428	Morrison	Daniel	pltf/exor	Certiorari	Sept 1812	motion to dismiss cert. / cont'd
p107	#428	Morrison	Isaac	deceased		Dec 1812	cont'd
p107	#428	Campbell	Michael	deft/exor		May 1813	cont'd // Cause removed / See #74
p107	#428	Phillips	Phillip	deceased			
p107							
p107	#429	Baxter	James & Co.	plaintiff	case appeal	Sept 1812	cont'd

MERO DISTRICT SUPERIOR COURT - 1810 - 1813

p107	#429	Bell	Hugh L.?	pltf/adm.		Dec 1812	cont'd
p107	#429	Nelson	Rob't	deceased		May 1813	jury/find for pltfs/assess his damages to $214.75 & costs
p108	#430	Haywood	John	pltf/exor	case appeal	Sept 1812	cont'd
p108	#430	Turner	John	pltf/exor		Dec 1812	the appellaant by his attorney dismisses his app'l
p108	#430	Turner	Martha	pltf/exor			judgment of the county court affirmed
p108	#430	Turner	Jas.	deceased			
p108	#430	Rutherford	William	defendant			
p108							
p108	#431	Overton	John	plaintiff	debt appl	Sept 1812	cont'd
p108	#431	Boyd	William L.	deft/exor	plea/never exor	Dec 1812	cont'd
p108	#431	Ford	Drury	deceased		May 1813	cont'd on aff't of deft//Cause removed / See #75
p108							
p108	#432	Lytle	William, Junr	plaintiff	debt appl	Sept 1812	cont'd
p108	#432	Richardson	Alex.	plaintiff	plea/never exor	Dec 1812	cont'd
p108	#432	Boyd	William L.	deft/exor		May 1813	cont'd on appl of deft / Cause removed / See #76
p108	#432	Ford	Drury	deceased			
p108							

MERO DISTRICT SUPERIOR COURT - 1810 - 1813

p108	#433	Smith	John H.	plaintiff	debt appl	Sept 1812	on petition & aff't of deft ordered cause adjourned to the
p108	#433	Boyd	Richard	deft/exor	plea/never exor		next circuit court of the county of Wilson.
p108	#433	Ford	Drury	deceased			
p109	#434	Lytle	William, Junr	plaintiff	debt appl	Sept 1812	on petitition & affidavit of deft ordered this cause adjourned
p109	#434	Boyd	Richard	deft/exor	plea/never exor		to next circuit court of the county of Wilson
p109	#434	Ford	Drury	deceased			
p109							
p109	#435	Masterson	Thomas	plaintiff	debt appl	Sept 1812	pltf being dead order this suit be revised in name of exors
p109	#435	Washington	Thomas	pltf/exor		Dec 1812	cont'd
p109	#435	White	Chapman	pltf/exor		May 1813	jury/find for pltf $57.43 debt +12% interest & costs
p109	#435	Burnet	Geo	defendant			
p109	#435	Martin	Geo.	defts security			
p109							
p109	#436	Gratz	Simon	plaintiff	debt appl	Sept 1812	cont'd
p109	#436	Gratz	Hyman	plaintiff		Dec 1812	cont'd
p109	#436	Stump	Christopher	defendant		May 1813	cont'd //Cause removed / See #77
p109							
p109	#437	Hope	Sam'l	plaintiff	Cert.	Sept 1812	cont'd

MERO DISTRICT SUPERIOR COURT   -   1810 - 1813

p109	#437	Rutherford	William	defendant		Dec 1812	cont'd
p109						May 1813	cont'd // Cause removed, See #78
p110	#438	Darrack	James	plaintiff	debt appl	Sept 1812	cont'd
p110	#438	Bell	Hugh F.	defendant	pay't //issue	Dec 1812	cont'd
p110	#438	Bell	William	defendant		May 1813	plea withdrawn/judg't affirmed agst principal with 12% int.
p110							
p110	#439	Bosley	Beal	plaintiff	debt appl	Sept 1812	cont'd
p110	#439	Shute	Thomas	defendant	payment//issue	Dec 1812	cont'd
p110						May 1813	jury/verdict for pltf/$79.91 with 12% interest
p110							
p110	#440	Brown	William	plaintiff	debt appl	Sept 1812	cont'd
p110	#440	Haywood	John		pay't & issues	Dec 1812	cont'd
p110						May 1813	plea withdrawn/judg't affirmed//rule for new trial//
p110							rule discharged//pltf releases all except $464.26
p110	#441	Bustard	John	plaintiff	debt appl	Sept 1812	cont'd

153

MERO DISTRICT SUPERIOR COURT - 1810 - 1813

p110	#441	Curtis	James		payment/issues	Dec 1812	cont'd
p110						May 1813	plea withdrawn//payment affirmed
p111	#442	Christmas	Thomas	plaintiff	debt appl	Sept 1812	cont'd
p111	#442	Nichols	John	defendant	pay't/set off	Dec 1812	judg't confesses by deft for $581 with interest & costs
p111					repn & issues		
p111							
p111	#443	Porter	Thomas	plaintiff	debt appl	Sept 1812	cont'd
p111	#443	McDowell		plaintiff		Dec 1812	cont'd
p111	#443	Williamson	John L.	defendant		May 1813	cont'd // Cause removed - See #79
p111	#443	Maddox	Ellis	deft security			
p111	#443	McKernon	Bernard	deft security			
p111							
p111	#444	Hopper	Thomas	plaintiff	cert	Sept 1812	motion to dismiss & cont'd
p111	#444	Nelson	Andrew	defendant		Dec 1812	cont'd
p111	#444	Crook	Begnal	deft security		May 1813	ordered cert. be dismissed/judg't agst deft & securities
p111	#444	Hartley	Charles	deft security			for costs
p111							

MERO DISTRICT SUPERIOR COURT   -   1810 - 1813

p111	#445	Den	John	plaintiff	eject	Sept 1812	cont'd
p111	#445	Ross	Daniel [owner]	plaintiff		Dec 1812	cont'd
p111	#445	Lovell	James	defendant		May 1813	cont'd // Cause removed / See #80
p112	#446	Young	John	plaintiff	covenant	Sept 1812	cont'd
p112	#446	Stump	Frederick	defendant		Dec 1812	cont'd
p112						May 1813	cont'd // Cause removed / See #81
p112							
p112	#447	Den	John [lessee]	plaintiff	eject.	Sept 1812	cont'd
p112	#447	Ross	Daniel [owner]	plaintiff	plea/not guilty	Dec 1812	cont'd
p112	#447	Stuart	Charles	defendant		May 1813	cont'd // Cause removed / See #82
p112							
p112	#448	May	Francis	plaintiff	case	Sept 1812	cont'd
p112	#448	Stephens	Robert	defendant	plea/non asst	Dec 1812	cont'd
p112						May 1813	cont'd // Cause removed / See #83
p112							

MERO DISTRICT SUPERIOR COURT - 1810 - 1813

p112	#449	Moore	Edwin L.	plaintiff	divorce petition	Sept 1812	copy of petition filed/defts answer filed//cont'd
p112	#449	Moore	Polly	defendant		Dec 1812	petition dismissed//petitioner to pay costs
p113	#450	Goodwin	William	pltf [infant]	petition	Dec 1812	cont'd
p113	#450	Goodwin	Susannah	pltf [infant]		May 1813	judgment for $467.61 & costs
p113	#450	Goodwin	George	pltf [infant]			
p113	#450	Goodwin	Jane	pltf [infant]			
p113	#450	Lofton	Thomas [next friend]	guardian			
p113	#450	Goodwin	John				
p113							
p113	#451	Davidson Academy	President & Trustees	plaintiff	Super.	Dec 1812	cont'd
p113	#451	Coleman	Joseph	defendant		May 1813	cont'd // Cause removed / See #84
p113	#451	Demumbrune	Timothy	defendant			
p113	#451	Lewis	William T.	defendant			
p113	#451	Searcy	Bernard	defendant			
p113							
p113	#452	Whitlow	Coleman	plaintiff	Super.	Dec 1812	cont'd
p113	#452	Coleman	Joseph	defendant		May 1813	cont'd // Cause removed / See #85
p113	#452	Lewis	William T.	defendant			
p113	#452	Searcy	Bernard	defendant			

MERO DISTRICT SUPERIOR COURT - 1810 - 1813

p113							
p113	#453	Miller	James	plaintiff	in equity	Dec 1812	cont'd
p113	#453	Hutchings	Catherine & als	defendant	issues of fact	May 1813	cont'd // Cause removed / See #86
p114	#454	Hackley	Elliot	plaintiff	detinue	Dec 1812	cont'd
p114	#454	Whiteside	Jenken	defendant	plea/the negro is a free man	May 1813	cont'd // Cause removed / See #87
p114							
p114	#455	Hawkins	Wyatt	plaintiff	covenant appl	Dec 1812	cont'd
p114	#455	Bell	Hugh F.	deft/admr		May 1813	cont'd // Cause removed / See #88
p114	#455	Nelson	Robert	deceased			
p114							
p114	#456	Hall	Elisha S. & Co.	plaintiff	debt	Dec 1812	cont'd
p114	#456	Overton	Thomas	defendant		May 1813	jury/ verdict for pltf #361.97/judgt for costs only by consent of plaintiff
p114							
p114	#457	McAlister	Charles	plaintiff	debt appl	Dec 1812	cont'd
p114	#457	Sappington	Roger B.	defendant		May 1813	plea dismissed/judgt affirmed agst principal & interest

MERO DISTRICT SUPERIOR COURT - 1810 - 1813

						Dec	
p115	#458	Marr	William M.	plaintiff	Scifa appeal	1812	cont'd
p115	#458	Nowell	William	defendant		May 1813	pleas withdrawn/judgment
p115	#458	Bell	Hugh F.	defts bail			
p115							
p115	#459	Stump	Christopher	plaintiff	debt appl	Dec 1812	cont'd
p115	#459	Parker	David	pltf/exor		May 1813	cont'd // Cause removed / See #89
p115	#459	Parker	William	pltf/exor			
p115	#459	Lenear	Jno	pltf/exor			
p115	#459	Lenear	Wm	deceased			
p115							
p115	#460	Porter	Thomas	plaintiff	in error	Dec 1812	cont'd
p115	#460	Claiborne	Thomas A.	defendant	erroors assessed	May 1813	judg't of the County Ciurt reversed
p115							instructorions to admit the evidence by
p115							them was rejected
p115	#461	Hickman	Thomas	plaintiff	in error	Dec 1812	cont'd
p115	#461	Russell	James	plaintiff	errors assigned	May 1813	cont'd // Cause removed / See #90
p115	#461	Craige	Daniel	defendant			
p115							
p115	#462	McKernan	Bernard	plaintiff	on appeal	Dec 1812	cont'd

158

MERO DISTRICT SUPERIOR COURT - 1810 - 1813

p115	#462	Stout	Sam'l	plaintiff		May 1812	cont't // cont'd / Cause removed / See #91
p115	#462	Stout	V. D.	plaintiff			
p115	#462	Boyd	John	defendant			
p116	#463	Llewallen	Shadrack	plaintiff	eject	Dec 1812	cont'd
p116	#463	Llewallen	Abednigo	plaintiff		May 1813	cont'd / by consent of the parties this case is consolidated with the following
p116	#463	Erwin	Andrew	defendant			
p116							
p116	#464	Llewallen	Shadrack	plaintiff	ejectment	Dec 1812	cont'd
p116	#464	Llewallen	Abednigo	plaintiff		May 1813	cont'd // Cause removed / See #92
p116	#464	Childress	Thomas	defendant			
p116							
p116	#465	Llewallen	Shadrack	plaintiff	ejectment	Dec 1812	cont'd
p116	#465	Llewallen	Abednigo	plaintiff		May 1813	cont'd // Cause removed / See #92
p116	#465	Fletcher	Thomas H.	defendant			
p116							
p116	#466	Blythe	Samuel H.	plaintiff	case	Dec 1812	issue alias agst Speed / cont'd
p116	#466	Speed	John	defendant		May 1813	cont'd // Cause removed / See #93
p116	#466	Poyzer	George	defendant			

MERO DISTRICT SUPERIOR COURT - 1810 - 1813

							May	
p117	#467	Brooks	William	plaintiff	Scifa	1813	issue alias
p117	#467	Priestley	John	witness	[not found]		Cause removed // See #94
p117							
							May	
p117	#468	Brooks	William	plaintiff	Scifa	1813	Scifa dismissed/ deft assumes the costs
p117	#468	Craighead	John B.	witness			
p117							
							May	
p117	#469	Brooks	William	plaintiff	Scifa	1813	alias issued
p117	#469	Phillips	Davd	witness	[not found]		Cause removed / See #95
p117							
							May	
p117	#470	Brooks	William	plaintiff	Scifa	1813	alias issued
p117	#470	Forrest	Reuben	witness	[not found]		Cause removed // See #96
p117							
							May	
p117	#471	Hudson	Westley	plaintiff	Scifa	1813	alias to issue
p117	#471	Hudson	Richard	witness	[not found]		Cause removed // See #155
p117							
							May	dismissed by pltfs atty // judg't to pltf for
p117	#472	Hudson	Westley	plaintiff	Scifa	1813	costs
p117	#472	Holmes	William	witness	[made known]		
p117							
							May	
p117	#473	Thomas	Jesse W.	plaintiff	Scifa	1813	issue alias to Maury County
p117	#473	Glovers	Joshua	witness	[not found]		Cause removed // See #97
p117							

MERO DISTRICT SUPERIOR COURT - 1810 - 1813

p117	#474	Thomas	Jesse W.	plaintiff	Scifa		May 1813	issue alias to Maury County // Cause removed / See #98
p117	#474	Glover	Elenor	witness	[not found]			
p118	#475	Thomas	Jesse W.	plaintiff	Scifa		May 1813	dismissed by pltf/judg't for costs
p118	#475	Walton	Loughton T.	witness	[not found]			
p118								
p118	#476	White	Thomas	plaintiff	Scifa		May 1813	dismissed & deft assumes the costs/atty relinqueshes fee
p118	#476	Leneer	Buchanan	witness				
p118								
p118	#477	Lytle	William, Senr.	plaintiff	Scifa		May 1813	cont'd // Cause removed / See #99
p118	#477	Caruthers	Jas.	defendant	plea payment...			
p118	#477	Bradford	Thos. G.	defts bail				
p118								
p118	#478	Lytle	William, Senr.	plaintiff	Scifa		May 1813	cont'd // Cause removed / See #100
p118	#478	Caruthers	Thos.	defendant	plea payment...			
p118	#478	Bradford	Thos. G.	defts bail				
p118								
p118	#479	Sturgus	James A.	plaintiff	Scifa		May 1813	to go no further, Drake being dead
p118	#479	Shepherd	A.	defendant				
p118	#479	Drake	Robert	defts bail				
p118								

MERO DISTRICT SUPERIOR COURT - 1810 - 1813

p118	#480	Snead	James	pltf/admr	detinue	May 1813	on Petition of pltf order adjourned to next Williamson County Circuit Court
p118	#480	Deloach	Sam'l	deceased			
p118	#480	Hooper	Joseph	defendant			
p118	#480	Perkins	William	pltfs bail			
p118	#480	Childress	Thos.	defts bail			
p118	#480	Irwin	Jno.	defts bail			
p119	#481	McCutchen	James	plaintiff	cert	May 1813	cont'd Cause removed // See #101
p119	#481	Tolbot	Thos.	deft/exor			
p119	#481	Weakley	Robert	deft/exor			
p119	#481	McGavock	David	deft/exor			
p119	#481	Tolbot	Matthew	deceased			
p119							
p119	#482	White	Alexander	plaintiff	in error	May 1813	judg't confirmed
p119	#482	Trigg	William	defendant	errors assisgned		
p119							
p119	#483	Strother	John	plaintiff	in error	May 1813	motion by deft to dismiss the writ of error
p119	#483	Christie	William	defendant	errors assigned		Writ of error quashed/pltf in error to pay costs
p119							
p119	#484	Nash	Sarah	pltf/admx	debt appeal	May 1813	plea withdrawn/judg't affirmed
p119	#484	Nash	Dan'l	pltf/admr	plea/payment...		
p119	#484	Nash	William	deceased			

MERO DISTRICT SUPERIOR COURT - 1810 - 1813

p119	#484	Hinton	Jeremiah	defendant			
p119	#484	Parker	Isham A.				
p119							
p119	#485	Jackson	Jas.	plaintiff	debt appl	May 1813	plea withdrawn//judgment affirmed
p119	#485	Jackson	Washington	plaintiff	plea/payment...		
p119	#485	Hall	John C.	defendant			
p119							
p119	#486	Deaderick	Thomas	plaintiff	debt appl	May 1813	paid
p119	#486	Sitler	Isaac	plaintiff	plea/pay't & issue		
p119	#486	Nichols	John	defendant			
p120	#487	Ross	David	plaintiff	debt appl	May 1813	motion to dismiss the appeal/motion overruled //by consent
p120	#487	Jackson	Henry	defendant	plea/pay't & issue		this cause is adjourned to next Court of Errors & Appeals
p120							
p120	#488	Eastes	Ludwell B.	plaintiff	case appl	May 1813	cont'd // Cause removed / See #102
p120	#488	Tolbot	Eli	defendant	non asst & issue		
p120							
p120	#489	Porter	Thomas	plaintiff	case appl	May 1813	cont'd // Cause removed / See #103
p120	#489	McDowell	Alexander	plaintiff	non asst & issue		
p120	#489	Rutherford	William	defendant			
p120							

MERO DISTRICT SUPERIOR COURT - 1810 - 1813

p120	#490	Rivers	Thomas	plaintiff	debt appl	May 1813	jury//verdict for pltf for $293.96 debt/#31.51 damgs + costs
p120	#490	Bell	Montgomery	defendant			
p120							
p120	#491	Nash	Sarah	pltf/admx	debt appl	May 1813	plea withdrawn/judg't affirmed
p120	#491	Nash	Dan'l	pltf/admr	pay't & issues		
p120	#491	Nash	Wm	deceased			
p120	#491	Vaughn	Paul	defendant			
p120							
p120	#492	Den	John	lessee	in ejectment	May 1813	cont'd by consent//Cause removed / See #104
p120	#492	Trebble	Spilsby	plaintiff	not guilty/issue		[trans from Dickson Circuit Ct]
p120	#492	King	Samuel	defendant			
p120	#492	Roberts	Obediah				
p121	#493	Hickman	Thomas	plaintiff	case appl	May 1813	Cont'd // Cause removed / See #105
p121	#493	Nicholson	Elisha	defendant			
p121							
p121	#494	Davis	William	plaintiff	debt appl	May 1813	plea withdrawn/judgment
p121	#494	Nichols	John	defendant			
p121							
p121	#495	Bradford	Larkin	plaintiff	debt appl	May 1813	paid
p121	#495	Nichols	John	defendant			
p121	#495	Coble	Nicholas	defendant			

MERO DISTRICT SUPERIOR COURT - 1810 - 1813

p121							
p121	#496	Raymond	Nicholas	plaintiff	debt appl	May 1813	cont'd // Cause removed / See #106
p121	#496	Stothart	Robert	defendant	pay't ...		
p121	#496	Bell	George	defendant			
p121							
p121	#497	Bell	Hugh F.	plaintiff	debt appl	May 1813	cont'd // Cause removed / See #107
p121	#497	Nelson	Robert	deceased			
p121	#497	Childress	John	defendant			
p121							
p121	#498	Boyd	John	plaintiff	In Error	May 1813	cont'd by consent // Cause removed / See #108
p121	#498	Boyd	Richard	defendant	Errors asst		
p122	#499	Maxwell	James	plaintiff	In Error	May 1813	cont'd by consent // Cause removed / See #109
p122	#499	Boyd	Richard	defendant	errors asst		
p122							
p122	#500	Tait	William	plaintiff	In Error	May 1813	cont'd by consent // Cause removed / See #110
p122	#500	Boyd	Richard	defendant	errors asst		
p122							
p122	#501	Harman	Lewis	plaintiff	cert	May 1813	cont'd // Cause removed / See #111
p122	#501	Anderson	William P.	defendant			
p122							

MERO DISTRICT SUPERIOR COURT - 1810 - 1813

p122	#502	Metcalf	Hai	plaintiff	case	May 1813	cont'd // Cause removed / See #112
p122	#502	Gregory	Edmund	defendant			
p122							
p122	#503	Brittan	Abraham	plaintiff	case	May 1813	cont'd // Cause removed / See #113
p122	#503	Nichols	John	defendant			
p122	#503	Whiteside	J.	pltfs bail			
p122	#503	Denhan	John	defts bail			
p122	#503	Hart	Robt W.				
p122							
p122	#504	Jackson	Andrew	plaintiff	debt	May 1813	cont'd // Cause removed // See #114
p122	#504	Harney	Thomas	defendant			
p123	#505	Campbell	Mich'l	survivor/pltf	debt	May 1813	alias to issue [not found]//cont'd / Cause removed/See #115
p123	#505	Philips	P.	deceased			
p123	#505	Campbell	Mich'l	deceased			
p123	#505	Thompson	Jason	defendant			
p123							
p123	#506	Basyl	Elizman	defendant	debt	May 1813	cont'd // Cause removed / See #116
p123	#506	Basyl	Isaac	defendant			
p123	#506	Whiteside	J.	pltfs bail			
p123	#506	Shannon	Sam'l	defts bail			
p123	#506	Basham	Peter	defts bail			
p123							

MERO DISTRICT SUPERIOR COURT - 1810 - 1813

p123	#507	Blount	Willie [Gov'r]	plaintiff	debt	May 1813	judgment on motion of Thomas Crutcher, Treasurer for $129.22 the balance of the State Tax for 1811 & costs
p123	#507	Bradford	Benj'n	defendant			
p123	#507	Norville	Wm	security			
p123	#507	Ake	Joseph	security			
p123	#507	Drake	John	security			
p123	#507	Roberson	David	security			
p123							
p123	#508	Blount	Willie [Gov'r]	plaintiff	debt	May 1813	judgment on motion for $729.63 & costs
p123	#508	Bradford	Benj'n	deft/collector			
p123	#508	Cannon	Clement	security			
p123	#508	Cannon	Minor	security			
p123	#508	Hutchings	Lemuel	security			
p123	#508	Carothers	Wm	security			
p123	#508	Henry	Charles	security			
p123	#508	Terry	Kibble	security			
p123	#508	Doherty	Wm	security			
p123	#508	Salling	Henry	security			
p123							
p123	#509	Blount	Willie [Gov'r]	plaintiff	debt	May 1813	judgment on motion for $298.52 & costs
p123	#509	Howell	John	deft/collector			
p123	#509	Fry	Henry	security			
p123	#509	Young	James	security			
p123							

MERO DISTRICT SUPERIOR COURT - 1810 - 1813

p123	#510	Blount	Willie [Gov'r]	plaintiff	debt	May 1813	judgment on motion for $640.94 & costs
p123	#510	Howell	John	deft/collector			
p123	#510	Connell	Giles	security			
p123	#510	Willis	Plummer	security			
p123	#510	Pickering	Charles D.	security			
p124	#511	Blount	Willie [Gov'r]	plaintiff	debt	May 1813	judgment on motion for $77.64 & costs
p124	#511	Read	James	deft/collector			
p124	#511	Molton	Michael	security			
p124	#511	Ellis	Francis L.	security			
p124	#511	Pearsall	Edward	security			
p124	#511	Walker	John	security			
p124							
p124	#512	Blount	Willie [Gov'r]	plaintiff	debt	May 1813	judg't on motion for $441.02 & costs
p124	#512	Love	David	deft/collector			
p124							
p124	#513	Blount	Willie [Gov'r]	plaintiff	debt	May 1813	Judg't on motion for $267.20
p124	#513	Cook	Jos.	dec'd/coll'r			
p124	#513	Bedford	Jonas	security			
p124	#513	Billingsley	Walter	security			
p124	#513	Smith	Richard W.	security			
p124							
p124	#514	Jones	Edward	plaintiff		May 1813	order for cert // Cause removed / See #117

MERO DISTRICT SUPERIOR COURT - 1810 - 1813

p124	#514	Jones	Richard H.	defendant		
p124						
p124	#515	Hyde	Taxwell	plaintiff	petition for dist.	May 1813	order for the division of lands lying in Davidson County
p124	#515	Hyde	Richard	plaintiff			Cause removed // See #118
p124	#515	Hyde	Henry	plaintiff			
p124	#515	Hyde	Benj'n	plaintiff			
p124	#515	Hyde	Edmund	plaintiff			
p124	#515	Stump	John	plaintiff			
p124	#515	Stump	Rebecca, his wife	plaintiff			
p124	#515	Hyde	Rebecca	deft/widow			
p124							
p124	#516	Den	John	lessee	ejectment		
p124	#516	May	John	plaintiff			
p124	#516	Hughes	Champ	defendant			
p124	#516	Metcalf	John	pltfs bail			

MERO DISTRICT SUPERIOR COURT   -   1810 - 1813

INDEX

Adams
  Robert 128
Ake
  Joseph 167
Alderson
  Christopher 144
Alexander
  Parker & als 9
Allen
  David 97
  Drury M. 92, 118
  John 41
  Samuel 97
Anderson
  John . . . 63, 64, 74, 115-118, 124
  Nathaniel S. 62
  Patton 14, 27, 75, 94
  William P. 58, 94, 106,
  109, 129, 144-146, 166
  Wm P. . . . 96, 143, 145, 147, 148
Armstrong
  Jos. W. 95
  Martin [heirs of] 95
Atkinson
  George 144
Baird
  John 26
Baker
  Isaac 89, 93
Balance
  Joshua 71

Balch
  Alfred 90
Barfield
  Frederick 66
Barnes
  James, Jr 52
  James, Junr 89
  James, Senr 89
  Thomas 107
Barrow
  Willie 61, 115, 141
Barry
  R. D. 92
  Redmond D. 131
Basham
  Peter 167
Basyl
  Elizman 166
  Isaac 166
Baxter
  James & Co. 151
Bean
  Jesse 122
  Stephen 3
Beard
  Zebuland 106
Beasley
  Jesse 95
Beaty
  William 72
Beck

John 11, 92
  John E. 125, 131
Bedford
  John R. 10, 26, 71
  Jonas 168
  Thomas 53
  Thomas [heirs] 44
Bell
  George 43, 165
  Henry 20, 148
  Hugh 79
  Hugh F. . 137, 153, 157, 158, 165
  Hugh L. 151
  Montgomery . . . 6, 94, 105, 164
  Samuel 22, 90
  William 153
Bennet
  Peter 119
Benton
  Jesse 108
Betts
  William 4
Bevins
  Fielder 126
Billings
  William 109
  Wm 70
Billingsley
  Walter 169
Birdwell
  George 43

MERO DISTRICT SUPERIOR COURT - 1810 - 1813

Black
- John 39

Blackamore
- John 25

Blair
- John 123

Bland
- Arthur 9

Blevins
- Henry 39

Blount
- Willie . . . 121, 122, 132, 167, 168

Blythe
- Samuel H. 160

Boggs
- James 83

Bosley
- Beal 153
- John 32

Bowles
- John 68

Boyd
- John 159, 165
- Richard . . . 31, 55, 139, 152, 165
- William L. 151, 152

Bradford
- Benj'n 167
- Benjamin J. 45, 126, 130
- Larkin 165
- Thomas G. 136
- Thos. 97
- Thos. G. 96, 161
- William 26

Bradshaw
- William 106

Brady
- William 150

Brewer
- Allen 24
- Sterling 23, 24

Brien
- Edw'd 143
- Isaac 143
- William 143

Brittan
- Abraham 166

Brooks
- Arthur 136
- John 121, 136
- Matthew 136
- Matthew, Jr. 102
- Robert 136
- William 4, 160

Brown
- George 24
- Joseph 8
- William 134, 137, 153

Brunson
- John 60

Bryant
- Shaderick 74

Buchanan
- John 82

Buck
- John E. 118, 142

Buford
- Simeon 30

Simpson 87

Bullard
- Joseph 121

Burland
- Thomas 143-148
- Thomas M. 144-148

Burnet
- Geo 152

Burnett
- George 13

Burnett & Raymond 132

Burt
- Christopher 97

Bustard
- John 154

Bustard & Eastin 38, 103
Bustard & Easton 33

Butler
- Thomas R. 26

Byrnes
- James 30

Cabaness
- Charles 132

Cabiness
- Ch. 26
- Charles 20, 21, 66

Caffery
- John 18, 25

Cage
- Reuben 85

Cain
- Daniel & wife 48

Caison
- Charles S. 76

MERO DISTRICT SUPERIOR COURT - 1810 - 1813

Caldwell
William 85
Campbell
John 9
Mich'l 166
Mich'l 112
Michael 135, 150
Cannon
Clement 167
Minor 167
Cantrell
Stephen, Jr. 135
Carothers
Wm 167
Carrick
John M. 122
Carroll
William 142
Carron
Charles L. 70
Carson
Charles S. 109
Cartwright
David 86
Jacob 86
James 86
Robert 86
Thomas 86
Caruthers
Jas. 161
Thos. 161
Casey
Randolph 65

Casselberry
Joseph 121
Catlett
Hanson 12, 49
Champ
John 15
Chandler
Isaac 125
Chanis
James 74
Chasseze
Benj. 112
Cheatham
Archer 125
John B. 121
Childress
Henry 9, 149
John 133, 134, 165
John, Jr 47, 68
John, Jr. 96
N. G. 129
Nath'l G. 24
Nathaniel G. 141
Thomas 133, 159
Thos. 162
Childs
John 14
Christie
William 162
Christmas
Thomas 154
William 38, 54, 97
Chumbley
Joseph 91

Claiborne
Ferdinand L. 128
Thomas A. 20, 35, 49,
50, 80, 86, 100, 158
Clark
David 2, 123
Clay
John W. 84
Cobb
Joseph 130
Coble
Nicholas 165
Cockrell
John, Junr 64
Cockrill
John, Junr 13
Coleman
Joseph 14, 18, 19, 38, 64,
73, 107, 119, 156, 157
Compton
Richard 98
Connell
Giles 168
Connelly
Thomas 34
Cook
Jos. 168
Cooper
Edmond 65
Edmund 48
John 147
Copeland
Samuel 2

172

MERO DISTRICT SUPERIOR COURT - 1810 - 1813

Corothers
- James 96
- Thomas 96

Cox
- John L. 138
- John S. 91

Coxe
- Thos 108

Craighead
- Jno. B. 109
- John B. 45, 108, 111, 160
- Thomas B. 101

Cribbins
- William 16

Criddle
- John 33, 90, 91, 113, 115

Crook
- Begnal 155

Crosky
- George D. 76

Crow
- Joshua 140

Crutcher
- Thomas 100
- Thos 17

Cummins
- David & others 55

Curry
- Isaac 88
- R. B. 88

Curtis
- James 154

Dabney
- John 101

Darrack
- James 153

Davidson
- Nathan 83

Davidson Academy 19
- President & Trustees . 55, 102, 156

Davis
- Anthony & others 25
- John 71, 77
- Obed 108
- William 164

Dawns
- James P. 88, 113

Deaderick
- George M. 77
- Thos. 129

Deaderick & Sommerville ... 14, 80, 82

Deatheridge
- John 35, 65
- Thomas 35

Deloach
- Sam'l 162

Demoss
- Abraham 81, 112
- James 118
- John 94, 112
- Lewis 94, 100, 111

Demumbrune
- Timothy 4, 19, 156

Den 30
- John 9, 53, 55, 142, 143, 155, 164, 169

Denhan
- John 166

Dergin
- John 131

Dew
- Arthur 120
- Susannah 120

Dickenson
- Jno 108, 137
- Jno. 114

Dickinson
- Jno 8, 116-119, 142
- John 98, 115, 142
- Mr. 31

Dickson
- William 28

Dillon
- Isaac 18
- Nathan 18
- Thomas 75, 119
- William 18

Dismuke
- Daniel 115

Dixon
- Tilman 110
- William 92

Doak
- John 74
- Susanna 74

Docker
- Edmund 145

Doherty
- Wm 167

MERO DISTRICT SUPERIOR COURT - 1810 - 1813

Donahoe
John 107
Donelson
John 53
Donnally
John 108
Douglas
Henry 90
Douglass
Hugh 128
James 124
Dowling
Harris 104
Downs
James P. 84
William 113
Drake
Henry 32
John 75, 167
Robert 112, 162
Draper
Daniel 145
Drury
Richard 17
Duckham
Joseph 146
Dunn
Michael C. 39, 93
Dupree
James 116, 120
Nancy 120
Durkenson
Jacob 90

Dyer
Joel 97
Robert H. 122, 123
Eakin
Moses 34, 87
Earthman
Isaac 91
James 108
Sarah 91
Easley
William 34
East
Tarleton 27
Easten
Thomas 93, 112, 114
Wm 112
Eastes
Ludwell B. 163
Edmiston
William 25
Edmondson
Robert 51
Robt 106
William 13, 22, 52
Wm 116
Edwards
Adonejah 107
Gray 62
Thomas, Junr 107
Thomas, Senr 107
William 117
Elam
Robert 77

Elliott
Samuel & wife 27
Ellis
Francis L. 168
Joseph T. 50
Elliston
Hugh 112
Joseph T. 52, 149
Erwin
Andrew 159
John 69, 127
Joseph 60, 62, 68-70,
81, 108, 109, 111
Evans
Robert 59
Ewi
Alexander 59
Ewing 38
Alexander 46
Andrew 93, 113
Ealey 119
Nathan 93
Farmer
Thomas 45
Fausset
Richard 87
Ferguson
William 61
Figures
Matthew 129
Fleshart
Elizabeth 37
Francis 38

MERO DISTRICT SUPERIOR COURT - 1810 - 1813

Fletcher
    Thomas H. 159
Flint
    John 103
Flynn
    Thomas 28
Folks
    Burwell 46
Ford
    Drury 151, 152
Forrest
    Reuben 160
Foster
    Anthony 5, 38, 98
Fox
    Paulina F. 90
    Thomas 90
Francis
    Charles 5
    Thomas W. 3
Frazier
    James 25
Fry
    Henry 168
Fuller
    Nehemiah 68
Gamble
    Edmund 41
Garrett
    William 117
Germain
    William 18
German
    Robert 59

    Shaderick 59
Gibbs
    Thos. 31
Gilbert
    William 58
Gilliam
    Divirix 56
    Edy 56
Gist
    William 122
Glass
    John 133
Glovers
    Elenor 161
    Joshua 161
Goldsberry
    J. B. 128
Goodloe
    John M. 98, 100
    Robert 27
    William 27
Goodrich
    Edmund 141
    John 68, 141
Goodwin
    George 156
    Jane 156
    John 156
    Susannah 156
    William 156
Goodwyn
    Peterson 115
Gordon
    Allen 63

    John 10, 20, 33, 34, 51,
    53, 60, 63, 84, 102, 110, 115, 116,
    123, 147-149
Grant
    William 116
Gratz
    Hyman 152
    Simon 152
Graves
    William 81
Gray
    Jacob 108
    James 14
    Joseph 100
    Suckey 14
    Young A. 14
Green
    Benj 91
    Elisha 69
    Sherwood 97
Greer
    Joseph 130
Gregory
    Edmond 78
    Edmund 166
    Polly 78
Griffin
    John 122
Griggs
    Real 124
Grimes
    John A. 114
    Philip 40
    William 40

MERO DISTRICT SUPERIOR COURT - 1810 - 1813

Grundy
F. 97, 108, 109, 112, 114, 115, 128-130
Felix 86, 88, 97, 98, 112, 119, 141

Hackley
Elliot 157

Haggatt
John 89

Hale
James 107

Hall
Charles M. 67, 84
E. S. 82, 129
Elihu & Co. 103
Elisha S. & Co. 157
Jlai 67
John C. 163

Hamilton
James 2, 76, 77, 123
Jno B. 142

Hannis
Samuel 29

Hardiman
Thomas 36

Harding
Edward 138

Hardinge
Samuel A. 35

Harman
Lewis 166
Richard 125
Thomas 19, 20

Harney
Thomas . . 11, 12, 44, 90, 92, 166

Harris
Arch'd H. 26
Sampson 40
Tyree 120

Harrison
John 24

Hart
Robert W. 114
Robt W. 166

Hartley
Charles 112, 155

Harvey
Thos 113

Hawkins
Wyatt 157

Hayes
O. B. 94, 95, 130
Robert 40

Hays
Andrew 133
Robert 1

Haywood
J. 141
John 116, 151, 153

Heard
James 94

Helm
John 135

Henderson
James 146
William T. 150

Henry
Charles 167
John 107

Herrod
Barned 1

Hess
William 92

Hews
Wm T. 46

Hickman
Thomas 5, 78, 92, 104, 135, 158, 164
Thos 58
Thos. 134

Hilton
Dan'l 93

Hinnen
James 41

Hinton
Jeremiah 6, 142, 163

Hobbs
Joel 127

Hodge
Francis 75
James 98

Holmes
William 161

Hooker
Ann 97
Elizabeth 97
Nathan 97

Hooper
Joseph 35, 162
Joseph & wife 1

Hope
Sam'l 153

176

MERO DISTRICT SUPERIOR COURT - 1810 - 1813

Hopper
    Thomas 154
Horton
    Jonah 93
    Josiah 41, 102, 134
Howell
    John 168
Howser
    Jacob 133
Huckeby
    John 107
Hudnell
    Ezekiel 71
Hudson
    Richard 160
    Thomas 48, 83
    Westley 90, 160
Hughes
    Champ 169
    William 141
Hughs
    Robert 66
Hunt
    John W. 109
    William 5
Huston
    James 37
Hutchings
    Catherine & als 157
    John 5, 10, 67
    Lemuel 167
    Thos. 10
Hyde
    Benj'n 169
    Edmund 169
    Henry 58, 110, 111, 169
    Mary 72
    Rebecca 169
    Richard 111, 169
    Taxwell 169
Hynes
    And'w 142
Ingram
    Francis 132
    Henry 50
    Pines 26, 27, 66
    William 18, 66
Irvin
    John 35
Irwin
    Jno. 162
    John 5, 56
Ivey
    Frederick 32
Jackson
    Andrew 5, 10, 15, 28, 58, 66, 166
    Henry 92, 125, 141, 163
    James . 16, 59, 71, 118, 124, 136
    Jas 79
    Jas. 163
    Samuel 5, 15, 141
    Wash. 79
    Wash'n 71
    Washington 59, 118, 124, 137, 163
Jackson & Hutchings 84
Janny
    Abel 17, 18
Jenkins
    Nimrod 122
Johnson
    Exum 104
Johnston
    Alexander 29, 120
    Andrew 16
    Isaac 85
    John 120
Jones
    Edward 169
    Richard H. 169
    William 20
Jordan
    James 91
Joslin
    Benjamin 82, 118
Josten
    Benj. 107
    Benjamin 117
Jourdan
    Meredith 91
Kavanaugh
    Charles 12
Kearney
    Elijah 115
    Vernon 115
Kelton
    Wm 126, 127
Kenisse
    Edward 138
Kennedy & Calhoon 98

MERO DISTRICT SUPERIOR COURT - 1810 - 1813

Kerr
Joseph 128
Sam'l 11
Kibble
Walter 125
Kiefe
Margaret 2
Thomas 2
Kile
William 125
Kincaid
John 3
King
James 11, 13, 76
Samuel 164
William 121
Wm 11, 13
King, Carson & King 11, 12
Kintzing
Abraham 37
Kirkman
Thomas 35, 51
Lacy
Hopkins 57
Laird
Alexander 124
Lane
Jacob A. 122
Langster
Alexander 144
Lankester
Robert 146
Large
Ebenezer 41

John 41
Laurey
Alexander 122
LeGrand
Peter 123
Lemasters
Isaac 32
Lencar
Buchanan 108
Lenear
Jno 158
Wm 158
Leneer
Buchanan 161
Lesslie
William 72
Lesuere
Littlebury 97
Lewis
Charles G. 95
Joel 16
William S. 46
William T. 23, 29, 67, 72, 84,
85, 98, 140, 156, 157
Wm T. 97
Litton
Jasper 138
Susannah 138
Llewallen
Abednigo 159
Shadrack 159
Lofton
Thomas 156
William 54

Long
John 54
Joseph 54
Richard H. 54
Love
David 168
Lovell
James 40, 99, 155
Lyle
George 51, 149
Lynch
James 66
Lyon
Henry 87
Lytle
Archibald 49
William 16, 22, 23, 74
William, Jr. 54, 114
William, Junr 140, 151, 152
William, Senr 96, 161
William, Senr. 161
Wm., Jr. 109
Maclin
John 3
Maddox
Ellis 154
Maderson
Thos. 129
Mahan
Wm A. 124, 126
Malone
Booth 129

178

MERO DISTRICT SUPERIOR COURT - 1810 - 1813

Manifee
- James N. 32
- Jonas 109

Mannon
- Unity 27

Marr
- Geo M. 43
- George W. L. .. 8, 10, 45, 49, 136
- John 95
- William M. 158

Martin
- Geo 152

Masterson
- Thomas 152

Mathews
- James 76

Maxwell
- James 165
- Jesse 1

May
- Francis 52, 83, 149, 155
- John 169

Mayfield
- John 88

McAlister
- Charles 158
- Thomas 92

McAllister
- Garland 110

McBride
- Samuel 119

McBurland
- Thomas 143

McCance
- Matthew 128

McCarty
- John 85

McClung
- Hugh 78

McConnell
- John P. 117

McCreary
- Nathaniel 103
- Thomas 45

McCulloch
- Alexander 123

McCutchen
- James 162

McCutcheon
- Thos 87

McDaniel
- Clement 12, 126
- David 122

McDowell 154
- Alexander 164

McGavock 38
- D. 30
- David . 48, 61, 104, 107, 150, 162
- James 41-43, 142, 143

McGinissey
- John 73

McKean
- Joseph 4, 30

McKernan
- Bernard 159

McKernon
- Bernard 154

McLendon
- Dennis 76, 77

McNairy
- Boyd 131, 142
- John 30, 82
- N. A. 131
- Nath'l 64
- Nathaniel A. 66, 134

Mcpherson
- John 39

Merriman
- William & wife 91
- Wm 108

Metcalf
- Hai 166
- Ilai 79, 87
- Jlai 48, 67
- John 53, 169

Miller
- Jacob 150
- James 157
- Jane 150
- William 32

Mitchell
- John 24, 132
- William 122

Molloy
- Thomas 1, 93, 114

Molton
- Michael 168

Monroe
- David P. 72

MERO DISTRICT SUPERIOR COURT - 1810 - 1813

Moore
Edward 127
Edwin L. 156
Polly 156
Thos. 132

Morgan
Wm C. 130

Morrison
Daniel 150
Isaac 150

Morrow
John 119

Moseley
Jacob 61

Mulheron
James 93

Mulherron
James 113

Mullen
Jonah 74
Josiah 100
Mary 50
William 149
William S. 50

Mullin
William 62

Murphy
Aexander 21
Wm 107

Murry
John 40, 42

Napier
Rich'd C. 128
Richard 7

Richard C. 47
Thomas 17, 33, 95

Nash
Dan'l 163, 164
Sarah 163, 164
William 18, 163
Wm 164

Neale
John 146

Neilson
Charles B. 132
David 81

Nelson
Andrew 154
John 51, 60
Rob't 151
Robert 79, 157, 165
Thos 88

Newnam
John 131

Newnan
John 46, 80, 86

Nichols
David 92
John 18, 21, 52, 68,
107, 110, 120, 154, 163-166
John & others 72

Nicholson
Elisha 164

Niel
Thomas H. 130

Norris
Ezekiel 29

Norville
Wm 167

Nowell
William 158

Nusam
Eldridge 20, 116
Francis 116
William 24, 52

Nusem
Francis 59

O'Bannon
P. N. 94

Ogden
Benjamin 60

Olive
Abel 33

Oren
James 3

Overton
John 87, 93, 113, 151
Thomas 157
Thomas J. 8
Walter H. 45

Owen
Edmond 17
Jabez 36
Joshua 36
Nathan 36
Rich'd B. 77

Page
Absolom 102, 114

Palmer
Martin 99

Park
    Joseph 68
Parker
    David 158
    Isham A. 134, 163
    Jess 92
    William 158
    Wm 88
Parks
    Thomas 147
Pate
    Anthony 25
    Willeroy 25
Patterson
    Thomas 71
Paxton
    Isaac 105
Payne
    Matthew 79
Payton
    John 131
Pearsall
    Edward 168
Pearson
    John 144
Penfold
    John 143
Perkins
    Joseph 146
    Nicholas T. 56
    Philip 91
    Thomas H. 10, 140
    Thos. H. 149
    William 33, 138, 162

    Wright 146
Perry
    George 98
Petty
    Jefferson 129
    Marthy 129
Philips
    P. 166
Phillips
    Benjamin 17
    Charles S. 14
    Davd 160
    Eliza 138
    John 66
    Joseph 90
    Merrel 138
    Phillip 151
    William 121, 122
    Wm 92
Pickering
    Charles D. 168
    John T. 147
Pilcher
    Joshua 142
Pinkerton
    James & als 36
Pipkins
    Philip 123
Pitteway
    Hincky 122
Poole
    Jefferson 129
    Marthy 129

Porter
    Alexander 94
    Alexander, Junr 126
    Alexander, Senr 126
    Ambrose 68
    Thomas 105, 118,
    150, 154, 158, 164
    Thomas & Co. 63
    Thos 88
Potello
    Catherine 118
Poyzer
    George 67, 102, 139, 160
Priestley
    John 160
Prince
    Francis 41
Pritchard
    Richard P. 144
Probart
    Wm L. 88
Prout
    Joshua 124
Pryer
    Sam'l 67
Pryor
    Sam'l 135, 138
    Samuel 84
    Susannah 135
Puckett
    Edward 48
Pullain
    Drury 134

MERO DISTRICT SUPERIOR COURT - 1810 - 1813

Purnell
    William 115, 139, 140
Purvis
    Allen 63, 148
Quinn
    Michael C. 106

Rains
    John 14, 117, 118
    John, Jr. 52
    John, Junr 89
    Wm 89
Ralston
    Joseph 21
Ramsey
    Thomas 52
Raymond
    Nicholas 13, 165
Read
    James 168
Reaves
    Robert 13
Reed
    Moses 11
Reeves
    Robert C. 59
Renfro
    Robert 8
Resse
    Gustaves 81
Rice
    Joel 92
Richardson
    Alex 151

    Alex'r 109
    Alexander 64, 66, 76
    Elijah 123
Ringue
    James B. 131
Rivers
    Thomas 164
Roberson
    David 167
Roberts
    Obediah 164
    Thomas 105
    William 88
Robertson
    Christopher 89, 91
    Duncan 69
    Elijah [heirs] 39
    James 14, 57
    Sarah 57
    Sterling C. 127
    Thompson 130
    William B. 135, 142
    Wm 139
Robinson
    Samuel 43
Rochel
    William 35
Roper
    Rich'd 109
    William 52, 107, 134
    Wm 131
Roper/Rosser
    William 126
Ross

    Daniel 91, 128, 155
    David 163
Rowlandson
    Sam'l 143
Russell
    James 121, 159

Rutherford
    Thomas 28, 62
    William 33, 151, 153, 164
Ryland
    Thomas 66
Salling
    Henry 167
Salter
    Michael 47
Saltor
    Michael 104
Sample
    John & Co. 76
Sanders
    Edward 15
Sanderson
    Robert 45
Sapping
    Roger B. 17
Sappington
    Roger B. . . 22, 78, 101, 134, 158
Saunders
    John 115
Sayers
    Sampson 14

182

MERO DISTRICT SUPERIOR COURT - 1810 - 1813

Scales
- Henry 62
- Jos. 17
- Joseph 110

Schroeder
- Henry 138, 139

Scott
- Samuel 74
- William, Senr 2

Scruggs
- Finch 80, 99, 133

Searcy
- Bennet 24, 38, 57, 60, 64, 75, 89, 93, 148, 149
- Bernard 156, 157
- Robert ... 6, 28, 57, 58, 125, 148

Seawell
- Benjamin 21, 93, 130
- Benjamin, Senr 106
- Thomas 88
- Thos. 130

Sebastian
- Isaac 79

Sevier
- John 28, 58

Shackleford
- Thos 142

Shannon
- Sam'l 167

Shaw
- Terrence 101

Shelby
- Anthony B. 87
- David 72, 82

Shepherd
- A. 162
- Adam 112

Sheppard
- Jacob 7

Shute
- Isaac 8
- John 8
- Thomas . 13, 22, 23, 54, 110, 153
- Thos 115
- Thos. 116

Simpson
- Sally 109

Sitler
- Isaac 163

Skinner
- Nathan 6

Slade
- Jeremiah 106

Smith
- John 38
- John H. 140, 152
- John H. & Co. 11, 67
- Richard W. 169
- Robert 48
- William 146
- Wm 95

Snead
- James 162

Sneed
- William 1

Somer
- Joseph 143

Sommerville
- John 20, 49, 148

Speed
- John 160

Spickard
- Jacob 106

Stapleton
- George 50

Statler
- Cornelius 132

Stephens
- Lewis 13
- Robert 83, 132, 155

Stewart
- Peter B. 73, 123
- William 73

Stone
- William 134

Stothart
- R. 4
- Robert 13, 165
- Robt 132

Stout
- Sam'l 159
- V. D. 159

Strother
- John 162

Stuart
- Charles 155
- Thomas 30, 53

MERO DISTRICT SUPERIOR COURT - 1810 - 1813

Stump

C. 72, 82

C. & Co. 40

Christopher 6, 7, 15, 47, 152, 158

Frederick 141, 155

John 6, 11, 36, 37, 47, 68, 69, 90, 127, 136, 140, 169

Rebecca 169

Sturgus

James A. 112, 162

Sugg

Jonah 81

Sulivan

Clemen 60

Sumner

Joseph 87

Tait

William . 24, 30, 38, 102, 149, 165

Wm 89, 115-117

Talbot 38

Clayton 113

Matthew 61

Thomas 30, 44, 61, 63, 143

Tate

Alexander 62

Tatum

Howel 55

Tayler

Joseph, Senr 111

Taylor

David 144

Sam'l 141

Teel

Edw'd 130

Tennison

Samuel 91

Tennisson

Sam'l 112

Samuel 94

Terrill

James 128

Terry

Kibble 167

Susannah 84

William 83

Thomas

Jesse 99, 133

Jesse W. . . 89, 99, 114, 133, 161

Mary 99

Phinehas 133

Phinihas 99

Richard 39

Robert 3, 8

Thompson

Jacob 94

Jason 166

Neil 6

Robt 82

Thornton

Samuel 113

Thurmon

John 107

Tiernan

Luke 137

Tipton

Edward 99

Rebecca 99

Titus

James 22

Tolar

Robert 121

Tolbot

Eli 163

Matthew 162

Thos 162

Trammell

Garrard 16

Trebble

Spilsby 164

Trice

John 106

Trigg

William 162

William, Junr 131

Trimble

David 8

John 8

Turner

Jas. 151

John 144, 151

Joseph 31

Martha 151

Skinner 145

William 91, 142

Turnstall

Edward 130

Tyree

Richardson 87, 113

Tyrrell

James 11, 128

MERO DISTRICT SUPERIOR COURT - 1810 - 1813

Vaughn
    Paul 164
Wade
    George 23, 92
    Judith L. 124
    William H. 124
Waggaman
    Thomas E. 47, 63, 67, 69, 70
Waggamand
    Thomas E. 60
Waggeman
    Thomas 16
Waggoner
    Michael 115
Walker
    John 168
    Matthew P. 90
    Peter & wife 36
    Phillip 21
Waller
    Thos 88
Walton
    Loughton T. 161
Ward
    Joseph 104
Warmack
    Archer 114
Washington
    Elizabeth 57
    Gray 57
    Thomas 57, 152
Watkins
    Isaac 139
    Thomas G. 12, 22, 141

Watson
    James 40
    Thomas 103
Weakley
    Robert 73, 131, 162
    Robt 61
West
    Geo 117
    Geo. 118
Westley
    Sam'l 15
Wharton
    J 110
    J. 110, 111, 115, 130
    Jesse 8
White
    Alexander 162
    Chapman 152
    John 88, 90, 122, 129
    Thomas 89, 161
Whiteside 33
    Geo. 145
    J. 109, 166, 167
    Jenken 157
    Jenkin 125, 130
    Jinken 79, 100
Whitfield
    Harrison 36
Whitlow
    Coleman 19, 156
Whittle
    Fortescue 71

Wiggen
    Thos. D. 121
Wiggin
    John P. 30
Wiggins
    Joseph & als 14
Wilks
    John 116
    Joseph 65
Williams
    Daniel 15
    John 65
    L. 89
    Lemuel 33
    Littlebury 64
    Nath'l W. 39
    O. 15
    Oliver 29
    Robert C. 150
    Sam'l W. 90
    Sampson 29, 58
    Thomas 145
Williamson
    Benjamin 72
    John L. 148, 154
    John S. 49, 97, 124, 131
    Thos. 132
Willis
    Plummer 168
Wills
    Benjamin D. 7
    Elias 7

MERO DISTRICT SUPERIOR COURT   -   1810 - 1813

Wilson
    James 127
    John, Junr 147
    John, Senr 147
    Nicholas 142, 148
    William 29
Winchester & Cage 130
Windfield
    Joseph 121
Winn
    Braxton B. 23
Witherspoon
    John 8
Wood
    Samuel 17, 18
    Titus 30, 31
Wright
    Abraham 70
    Elizabeth 102, 105
    John 102, 105
    William 28
Wyche
    Nathaniel 65
York
    William 56
Young
    Daniel 127
    James 168
    Jno. L. 115
    John 155
    John L. 48, 127

Other Books by the Author:

Davidson County, Tennessee Deed Book H, 1809-1821
Davidson County, Tennessee Deed Books T and W, 1829-1835
Davidson County, Tennessee Deed Book Z: Personal Property Deeds, September 5, 1835-January 2, 1838
Davidson County, Tennessee Naturalization Records, 1803-1906
Superior Court of Law and Equity, Mero District of Tennessee, 1803-1805 (Middle Tennessee)
Superior Court of Law and Equity, Mero District of Tennessee, 1806-1809 (Middle Tennessee)

CD: Davidson County, Tennessee Deed Book P: Personal Property Deeds, 15 November 1821-13 February 1829 and Deed Books T and W, 1829-1835

www.ingramcontent.com/pod-product-compliance
Lightning Source LLC
Chambersburg PA
CBHW081842230426
43669CB00018B/2787